DISCOVERING
PAUL

Dedicated to
Mr William A. Wigney
pastor, evangelist, tentmaker,
who challenged us to the work
of the ministry

DISCOVERING
PAUL

Gordon Moyes
Photographs by
John Graham

An Albatross Book

© Gordon Moyes 1986

Published in Australia and New Zealand by
Albatross Books Pty Ltd
PO Box 320, Sutherland
NSW 2232, Australia
and in the United Kingdom by
Lion Publishing
Icknield Way, Tring
Herts HP23 4LE, England

First edition 1986

National Library of Australia
Cataloguing-in-Publication data

Moyes, Gordon, 1938
Discovering Paul

Simultaneously published: Tring, Herts:
Lion Publishing

Bibliography
ISBN 0 86760 006 3 (Albatross)
ISBN 0 7459 1190 0 (Lion)

1. Paul, the Apostle, Saint. 2. Christian
saints — Turkey — Tarsus — Biography.
I. Title
225.9'24

Typeset by Rochester Photosetting Service, Sydney
Printed by Mandarin Offset Marketing (HK) Ltd, Hong Kong

Contents

Acknowledgements

I would like to thank my
secretary, Jan Fishburn, who
worked on typings and retypings;
Ron Schepis, my son-in-law, who
helped with the archeological
research; my colleague Rev. Dr
Tony Chi for preparing the
weekly Bible readings; my
publisher John Waterhouse whose
encouragement and expertise in
editing and overseeing the
production of this series has won
him awards from his peers; the
crew of Wesley Film Productions
who made the trips throughout
the Mediterranean so memorable;
the Australian Christians who
invested $1 million in making the
series a reality; Rev. John Graham
who took the still photographs
that have enhanced these books;
and my wife Beverley and our
four children who over the years
have encouraged and stimulated
me in walking with the apostle
Paul.

By the same author:

Discovering Jesus
12 Steps to Serenity
Mission On
Be a Winner!
Confidence in Time of Trouble
The Secret of Confident Living
How to Grow an Australian Church

Introduction

There is no writer known to history before St Paul who confronts us so directly in his work, and hardly any since. Why then do we need to discover him?

Oddly enough, direct contact with another person can be as baffling as it is revealing. That is why most people shroud themselves in a conventional form of expression. It makes communication easier — in a superficial sense. Historians also like to work by stereotypes, reducing puzzling individualities to familiar patterns. Personal contact, through 'primary' sources, is a demanding experience, whether in history or any other

Theatre at Delphi: Greece

form of human encounter.

In the centuries-long tradition of Greek literature, Paul's letters come as an abrupt shock. We can see that those who first read them were also shocked. Instead of the elegant and studied presentation expected of a respectable scholar, he simply poured out his response to the crises of life in his churches in a way that was both humiliatingly intimate and at the same time liberating in its vivid display of thought and emotion.

No amount of learned analysis will get to the bottom of this. It is a personal form of communication that can only be fully explored personally. Gordon Moyes has graphically set out his own encounter with the ancient Paul. It is inspired by his modern experience as a minister and evangelist. But it also anchors Paul in the world of his day. A full understanding of another person requires sympathetic awareness of his life and circumstances. Gordon Moyes provides us with a whole series of ways into the world and mind of Paul.

It can be a transforming encounter. I first read the letters of Paul thoroughly while sitting in the scripture class in a New Zealand high school. In those days we had to read scripture individually and in silence. No comment was allowed. Stultifying as this might seem to an educationist, the knowledge gained has proved for me a lasting fascination. Now as a professional student of history I can see a remarkable thing about it. Across the centuries so many millions have entered into the same relationship with Paul that his imprint lies deep within our whole tradition of civilisation.

The idea that our culture has somehow been dechristianised, or needs to be, has become a voguish one, but like any fashion it looks to externals only. For who is there today who does not object to self-importance? Who is there who does not admire self-sacrifice? Who does not value commitment and regret apathy? Who does not believe we can be changed for the better? Who does not think that consistency between human motive and action is important? In terms of cultural history, we all owe these basic ideals ultimately to Paul, whether we recognise it or not. Most people who think the message of Paul outmoded would be devastated if they lost the values he has supplied them with.

This book is an invitation to the modern world to discover or re-discover its vital roots through a meeting with Paul that is both historical and direct. Many will be grateful to Gordon Moyes, as I am, for the authentic way he has opened up this opportunity.

Professor E.A. Judge
School of Ancient History
Macquarie University
Australia

1

Paul the Pharisee

Henry Kissinger, in the mid-1970s, gave occasion to the term 'shuttle diplomacy' as he moved between the major powers of our world seeking peace and easing international tension.

Shuttle diplomacy could perhaps describe some of the influences in the first century of the apostle Paul. What he did then, put into our terms, would be equivalent to travelling around the world debating with the Russians in Russian concerning their philosophy of history, lecturing the Chinese in Chinese on their use of power and disputing with the Americans in English on their moral standards — and forming, everywhere he went, multi-cultural communities which would affect the future history of the world. Within two hundred years of his death, what he had done would be recognised as the pervasive force within the world.

Such was the influence of the apostle Paul.

Put this into the context of a remarkable conversion, of a complete theological turnaround, of courage demonstrated in the face of frequent riots, of physical punishment, beatings and imprisonments, and of personal catastrophe such as shipwreck, and we begin to sense the variety of Paul's life. He became at the one time one of the most influential figures this world has ever seen, second only to Jesus himself in his influence upon Christianity, while at the same time becoming one of the most controversial of all theologians.

Adolf Hitler once said of Paul: 'Christ was an Aryan. But Paul used his teaching to mobilise the underworld and to organise an earlier Bolshevism.' Hitler was following his mentor, Frederick Nietzche, who in turn had said: 'A God who died for our sins; redemption through faith; resurrection after death — all these are counterfeits of true Christianity, for which that disastrous, wrong-headed fellow Paul must be held responsible.'

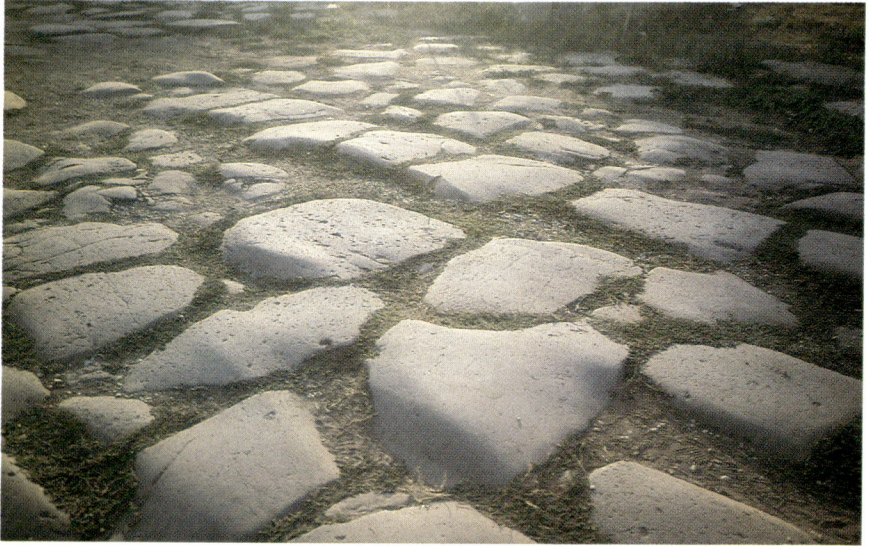

Over the years people have blamed Paul for everything. 'St Paul would almost certainly have condemned tobacco if he had know of its existence,' said Bishop Samuel Butler. The English philosopher, John Stuart Mill, commented: 'I hold St Paul to have been the first great corrupter of Christianity.' The German psychologist, Carl Jung, said: 'It is frankly disappointing to see how Paul hardly ever allows the real Jesus of Nazareth to get a word in.'

As opposed to these comments, consider Dean W.R. Inge: 'To the historian there must always be something astounding in the magnitude of the task Paul set himself, and in his enormous success. The future history of the civilised world for 2,000 years, perhaps for all time, was determined by his missionary journeys and his hurried writings.' And as another theologian has said: 'There has probably seldom been anyone at the same time

hated with such fiery hatred and loved with such passion as Paul.'

How can we in this twentieth century understand the influence of such a controversial man? What made Paul what he was?

There are perhaps five influences making each of us what we are: family background and heredity; early upbringing and environment; education; God's intervention in our lives; and our personal response to all these. We will look at Paul's life in each of these areas to discover who he was. Before examining these, however, we should answer the question: how do we know about Paul anyway?

Paul is not known outside of the New Testament; there are no writings by Greek, Jewish or Roman scholars about him during his lifetime. The authors of the day did not notice his profound influence and, indeed, it took three centuries before the impact of his work was such as to change the history of the Roman world.

Sources of information on Paul

There are only two sources for our information on Paul: the letters he wrote, which are important primary sources, and a history of the early church written by Luke which we know as 'The Acts of the Apostles'.

1. His letters

The letters of Paul were particularly personal, yet written as an official statement for public reading. Even the personally addressed letters, such as the letter to Philemon, were also addressed 'to the church that meets in your house'.[1]

One of his letters, that to the Romans, was a carefully constructed treatise, yet even this long and carefully argued theological presentation had a personal purpose.[2]

As Bishop J.B. Lightfoot said: 'In the whole range of literature there is nothing like St Paul's letters. Other correspondents may be more voluminous, more elaborate, more studiously demonstrative. But none is so faithful a mirror of the writer.'

The letters of Paul were typical in their construction to that of other letters in the ancient world. They started with the salutation to the recipient, mentioned the name of the sender (how much more sensible than our modern practice of leaving the name of the sender until the end of the letter), presented a greeting and a thanksgiving to the recipient, and concluded with some personal information and final signature.

Paul used to dictate his letters to a secretary or 'amanuensis' who would take down in a form of shorthand the dictation of

Paul, scribing with a stylus on a waxed tablet the notes which were then written in longhand, transcribed by pen and ink onto papyrus scrolls. Once the amanuensis identified himself as Tertius.[3] It is possible that Luke and Timothy also acted as secretary to Paul. However, Paul always personally signed his letters — as he indicated a number of times.[4]

Thirteen of the letters in the New Testament have Paul's name on them. While some theologians think that the personal letters to Timothy and Titus were written by a disciple of Paul, I would accept that all of the thirteen letters were written by him personally. The letter to the Hebrews, which was ascribed in the King James Version as being a letter of Paul, is universally accepted now as being written by someone else.

Paul's letters have a number of features. There are some very carefully written passages, such as in Romans 1:16-17 where his theme for the whole letter is spelt out and developed over the next eight chapters. Sometimes Paul breaks into the most beautiful of lyrical writing, such as the great chapter on love.[5] However, these lyrical passages have been found by scholars to be very careful in their construction. Paul used *chiasmus* — the lyrical device of developing a theme in one sentence word-by-word, then reversing the order in the remaining half of the sentence (look, for example, at 1 Thessalonians 2:19-20). Some scholars have identified many places where the form of Paul's sentence goes abc-cba.

Paul frequently quoted other authors, even on occasions quoting hymns from the early church. One such hymn is found in the great passage on the incarnation of Christ;[6] another is in his letter to Timothy, where he encouraged loyalty to Christ.[7] When he addressed the philosophers in Athens, he quoted Greek poets and quoted on other occasions extensively from the Old Testament.

Some of his letters have passages which could be summaries of sermons that he had given outlining the true consequences of the Old Testament law. The balance between law and faith as found in Galatians (chapters 3 and 4) could quite easily have been a sermon summary.

Frequently, Paul concluded his letters with a number of personal exhortations to live a lifestyle consistent with the teachings of Jesus.[8] Yet in everything Paul wrote, there is one central theme that he constantly returned to no matter what subject he was writing about: the centrality of Jesus Christ. To be 'in Christ' was to give a totally new world view, a new way of living, and a new standard of personal faith and conduct. Everything changes when we become members of his body.

In the past decade, scholars have tended to support the more traditional views of the authorship of Paul's letters. Statistical analysis of the use of his particular phrases, key words and sentence structures — even down to the use of conjunctions like 'and' and 'but' — have found the grammatical and vocabulary styles of each letter to be consistent with that found in the majority.

2. The Acts of the Apostles

The historian Luke wrote not only the Gospel which bears his name but the Acts of the Apostles as well. He did not repeat the details of the letters of Paul when, after Paul's death, he wrote his history of the early church. While there are a few similarities with the letters of Paul, there are no direct quotes and the few similarities in wordage can be accounted for by being about the same subject. While we have none of the original copies of Paul's letters to check, Luke's knowledge of them may have been firsthand — from his role as an amanuensis, or from hearing them read in the churches he attended.

The Acts of the Apostles is our best secondary source on the life and teaching of Paul, helping us with our understanding of the sequence of the events in Paul's life. Unfortunately, the New Testament arranges the letters of Paul in order of their length: first to churches, then to individuals. Acts, however, helps us to arrange the letters in *chronological* sequence with his life.

According to the Acts of the Apostles, Paul's life centred around three trips to Jerusalem after his conversion, three journeys round the Mediterranean world and one long trip to Rome in his legal appeal to Caesar. Because the focus of Acts is primarily on the geographic expansion of Christianity, we have no biography of Paul in the sense that we have in the Gospels of the life of Jesus.

The Acts of the Apostles is an account of how the Christian church grew from its Jewish origins in Jerusalem by an author who, for the most part, was present with Paul during a dramatic period of Paul's ministry. Luke's presence is signalled by his sudden use of the term 'we' in passages indicating that he was there with Paul at the time.[9] As for the rest of the material covering those times when Luke himself was not present, he obviously selected it from his personal research as he did with his Gospel.[10]

Dome of the Rock: Jerusalem

Luke follows the sequence of Acts 1:8. The early Christians were to be witnesses to Jesus throughout Jerusalem, Judea, Samaria and then to the ends of the earth. The book of Acts is actually broken into four sections where Luke indicates the expansion of Christianity from Jerusalem to Judea and Samaria, and finally to Rome. Each of these sections concludes with a summary of how, through faith and the power of the Holy Spirit, the gospel spread throughout the known world.[11]

Portico of St Peter's Basilica: Rome

The early part of Acts focuses on significant people in the early church: the apostles Peter and John, the first Christian martyr Stephen, the evangelist Philip and then the story of Saul who became Paul. The rest of the book of Acts centres on Paul and his activities, even though the other apostles were still active. Peter's journeys, for example, were quite impressive, but we have no written record of his preaching, teaching or ministry after the early chapters in Acts simply because he did not have an amanuensis with him like Paul. Two letters written late in his life are all we possess.

Paul's visits to Jerusalem are difficult to fit in with any timetable based on the information found from the letters. The fact is we have not sufficient information for an exact chronology of either the life and travels of Paul, or of the sequence of his letters. Many have tried and have twisted either the letters or the Acts of the Apostles to suit their framework. The fact is it is not possible to recover an exact sequence of either activities or writings.

The early life of Paul

Based then upon these significant primary and secondary source documents, what do we know about Paul's early life?

1. Family background

Paul would have had three names: his forename, his family name and an additional name (his *praenomen, nomen* and *cognomen.*) We do not know Paul's family name although his forename would have been Saul, Latinised into Paul.

His father was a Jewish community-leader and a Roman citizen. Citizenship was conferred by Romans upon distinguished local people in the provinces who helped Rome in its governing of a community or conquering of it. Tarsus was a major Roman provincial centre governed under generals including Pompey and Antony. Paul's father, or possibly his grandfather, performed some meritorious service to the Romans. As the family business was tentmaking, perhaps he provided the tents in large numbers for the army.

Paul was taught a trade as was customary with all Jewish boys, even though he would have belonged to a fairly affluent or at least a middle-class family. Paul once spoke with a sense of pride of his own achievements as a worker: 'You yourselves know that I have worked with these hands of mine to provide everything that my companions and I have needed'.[12] This is not the comment of a labourer, but the comment of an intellectual proud of the fact that he could be independent due to his skill with his hands.

His early life, Paul believed, was marked out by God for a special purpose. In Galatians he used the following ideas of Jeremiah: 'I chose you before I gave you life, and before you were born I selected you to be a prophet to the nations'.[13] Paul was born about 3 or 4 BC. His death occurred probably in his sixty-eighth year. He was proud of the fact that his family tradition was as correct and privileged in the Jewish faith as any:

I was circumcised when I was a week old I am an Israelite by birth, of the tribe of Benjamin, a pure-blooded Hebrew. As far as keeping the Jewish Law is concerned, I was a Pharisee, and I was so zealous that I persecuted the church. As far as a person can be right by obeying the commands of the Law, I was without fault.[14]

He was called Saul after the most outstanding of his forefathers, the first king of Israel, who belonged to the same tribe. Living in a Roman-governed, Greek-speaking city posed problems for an orthodox Jew like Paul. In practice, he would need to be *tri*-lingual. At synagogue school he would learn Hebrew from the local rabbi. Travelling to Jerusalem, he would have spoken Aramaic, the Semitic language which originally came from Syria. He would also be fluent in Greek, the common language of the world of his day.

There was a fourth language in widespread use at the time: Latin. The sign on the cross of Jesus, 'This is the King of the Jews', was in Greek, Latin and Hebrew. Citizenship enabled Paul to have free and unfettered travel throughout the Roman Empire, giving him the privilege of a fair public trial (when accused) and providing him with protection many times during his life. The Romans put to death any who claimed citizenship falsely. A citizen usually carried a small tablet which acted as a birth certificate, giving his birth registration and number. Paul's citizenship was the passport to the Roman Empire.

Roman citizenship was a tremendous privilege. The military tribune's words in Jerusalem indicated how he envied Paul's acquiring of citizenship by birth: 'I became a citizen by paying a large amount of money'.[15]

2. Early environment
Paul once stated: 'I am a Jew, born in Tarsus in Cilicia, a citizen of an important city.[16]

Tarsus was one of three university cities of the ancient world, the other two being Athens and Alexandria. As a busy seaport, it became a key trading centre for caravans of camels from both east and west. The Jews of the community lived in their own part of the town, by the river Cyndus. As a Roman citizen from a Greek city with a Jewish education, Paul had unique credentials that fitted him for leadership within the Christian church.

In the mountains round Tarsus the goats were kept for their hair which made a waterproof cloth called cilicium. Giving good protection against heat and rain, this material was used to make tents, and was famous for its durability. It is possible that Paul's father or grandfather had founded the firm of tentmakers in the city. Its university was filled with students — including those from other centres. Augustus Caesar had been a student in this cosmopolitan university city.

Today, the Roman town of Tarsus lies buried beneath the modern town. Archeological excavations since 1947 have unearthed a number of significant Roman mosaics. There is a small Roman theatre, the remains of a temple and large public buildings — possibly connected with the university.

In Paul's day, the city may have had a population of close to 500,000. It had a history that went back to the second millennium BC. It is well-known in ancient literature. Many writers recorded the visits of Cyrus the Younger and Alexander the Great. The Greek historian, Xenophon, described in great detail the curing of illness in Tarsus, praising the city for its culture and medical facilities four centuries before Paul. Forty years before Paul's birth, Cleopatra reputedly sailed there from Egypt to meet Mark Antony, Roman General for the province. It was there one of their famous love scenes, celebrated by Shakespeare, was played out.

Greek culture pervaded the Roman Empire. The Roman orator Horace once commented, 'Captive Greece took Rome captive'. From the second century when tens of thousands of Greek prisoners were brought back to Rome as slaves, their language, philosophy and culture dominated the Roman Empire. The *Koine* or common Greek became the language of communication throughout the Roman Empire. The Greek mystery religions were Romanised, the early beliefs about Dionysius, Aphrodite, Zeus and Artemis all being mentioned during the travels and preaching of Paul.

The Jewish religion was the most consistent yet exclusive within the known world. Based upon the Mosaic Law, the followers of the one God Jehovah kept their racial identity pure, while their distinctive dress, diet and habits set them apart. Some of the Jewish community looked for a coming Messiah who would redeem them from their sins and free them from their political lords.

Cleopatra's Arch: Tarsus

Such was the multi-culturalism of this community that the young Paul would have been forced to mix with cultural Greeks and pragmatic Romans, with slaves and free men, with traders and sailors — all bringing with them traditions and customs from every corner of the known world. Little did Paul realise that this mixed cultural background would provide the stage on which he would play such an important part.

3. Education

Paul's education started at five years when he attended the synagogue school. There he began to learn by heart the Old Testament Law and to read the scriptures — probably in the Greek Septuagint, the Greek translation of the Old Testament. He frequently quoted from this translation. However, because his father was a Pharisee, Paul also learnt Hebrew, the exclusive language of the learned.

After his early schooling in Tarsus, Paul went for graduate studies at the feet of the most famous Pharisee of his day, Gamaliel, in Jerusalem. Gamaliel was head of the Hillel School of orthodox belief. The Hillel School was strictly orthodox. Gamaliel was a member of the Sanhedrin, acknowledged as a wise and careful counsellor. It was his advice to his fellow members of the Sanhedrin which led to the decision not to make martyrs of the early Christians.[17] While he was in Jerusalem, Paul probably lived with a relative. Later in his life he was warned by his sister's son of a plot against him.

The Pharisees developed as a party within orthodox Judaism shortly after the time of the revolt of Judas Maccabaeus against the Greek overlords in the middle of the second century BC. They were called 'the separated ones', separating themselves from other forms of religious belief within Judaism to be the 'godly people' known for their piety and correct obedience to the Law. They observed 365 commandments concerning the things they must not do, and around these added, like a hedge, a protective barrier of oral instruction and prohibition designed to protect themselves from inadvertently breaking the Law of God. They traced their origins to those spoken about by the prophet Malachi:

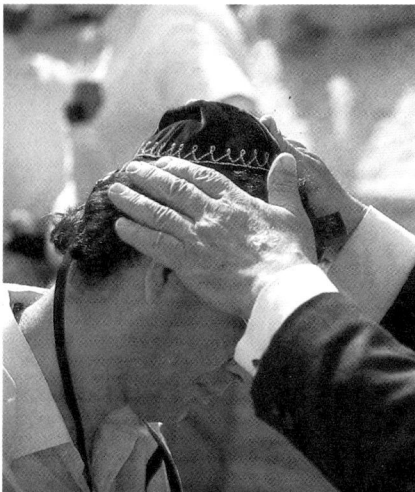

Then the people who feared the Lord spoke to one another and the Lord listened and heard what they said and in his presence there was written down in a book a record of those who feared the Lord and respected him. 'They will be my people,' says the Lord Almighty. 'On the day when I act, they will be my very own.'[18]

The Pharisees believed that they belonged to this chosen group who would be spared from the judgment of God. In the time of Jesus there were about 6,000 Pharisees out of two million people in all Palestine. The population of Jerusalem in the time of Jesus was 100,000, except during feast times like the Passover when crowds would have exceeded 500,000 persons.

Paul was proud of his training as a Pharisee. Following his training, he returned home to Tarsus for approximately six years. It was during this time he missed the most significant events in the history of Israel: the public ministry, death and resurrection of Jesus. Shortly afterwards, he returned to Israel and became a member of the Sanhedrin, a great honour for a young man of about thirty years.

The Sanhedrin was the supreme Jewish legal and civil court. Paul determined that as one of the upholders of the faith and traditions of his people he would make sure that all perverseness would be stamped out. He immediately became a persecutor of the Hellenistic Jews, those Jews who were so influenced by Greek culture that they had allowed their Greek culture to influence their Jewish faith: 'He also talked and disputed with the Greek-speaking Jews, but they tried to kill him'.[19]

This same zeal led Paul to seek permission from the council to stamp out the new heretics, the people of the Way:

I myself thought that I should do everything I could against the cause of Jesus of Nazareth. That is what I did in Jerusalem. I received authority from the chief priests and put many of God's people in prison; and when they were sentenced to death, I also voted against them. Many times I had them punished in the synagogues and tried to make them deny their faith. I was so furious with them that I even went to foreign cities to persecute them.[20]

It was at this point in Paul's life that God decided to intervene. God had other plans for Paul. He was to be his chosen messenger to take the gospel into the known world.

Despite problems of physical health which were to dog his tracks throughout his life, he always gave himself completely to the service of God. As a committed Pharisee determined to uphold the Jewish law, Paul opposed any who sought to change the traditions and customs of the Jews, whether the Hellenists (by adapting their religious faith to Greek influence) or the early Christians (by worshipping Jesus as the Messiah). After he had met the risen Christ, Paul saw Jesus as the fulfilment of all the Old Testament pointed to. The foe of the Christian faith became its friend; the persecutor became the preacher; the greatest adversary of the Christian faith became its greatest advocate.

Despite his family background, early environment and education, God intervened in Paul's life.

If you take your life and look back upon it, can you see God working a pattern through your family background, your early environment and your education? How does one respond to God's intervention? That's the theme to which we now turn.

For personal reading

Theme: Paul's rich heritage

MONDAY   Paul's Jewish upbringing
Acts 26:2-8

TUESDAY   Gamaliel's role in Paul's life
Acts 5:33-39

WEDNESDAY   Paul's education
Acts 22:1-5

THURSDAY   Paul, a Pharisee
Acts 23:1-10

FRIDAY   Paul, a Roman citizen
Acts 22:25-30

SATURDAY   Paul's authority based on the scriptures
Acts 13:16-25

SUNDAY   Paul's zeal
Acts 21:37-40 and Acts 22:1-3

For group study

Topic: The Variety of Paul's life

1 How did Paul influence his world?

2 What are the main personal letters of Paul?

3 How would you describe the construction of a 'typical' letter of Paul?

4 Could you describe some distinctive features in Paul's letters? Are they any different from a modern day personal letter?

5 How important would you say is one's family tradition and background?

6 Paul was influenced by the multi-cultural community in a Roman province, which was also the centre of a Greek culture. Describe how these factors, together with his religious upbringing, would later work in his life.

7 Who do you think you are? Do you see God at work in your childhood, youth and adult life?

2

Paul the Persecutor

Jesus rose from the dead. That changed everything. The resurrection fact released with power a resurrection faith.

The early preaching
The early Christians, inspired by the example of Peter and John, proclaimed the gospel everywhere. Although they had no fixed message, their preaching contained frequent repetitions of the same theme.

When Paul wrote to the church at Corinth, he possibly repeated one of the early creeds:

I passed on to you what I received, which is of the greatest importance: that Christ died for our sins, as written in the scriptures; that he was buried and that he was raised to life three days later, as written in the scriptures; that he appeared to Peter and then to all twelve apostles. Then he appeared to more than five hundred of his followers at once, most of whom are still alive, although some have died. Then he appeared to James, and afterward to all of the apostles. Last of all he appeared also to me.[1]

This passage, the various sermons in the book of Acts and the shape of Mark's Gospel, led the British scholar C.H. Dodd to conclude that there were six basic elements in the early apostolic preaching:

* The age of the kingdom is at hand.
* It has been fulfilled in the life, death and resurrection and. ascension of Jesus.
* Jesus is the Messiah reigning at God's right hand.
* The Holy Spirit in the church is the sign of Jesus' power.
* The Messiah will come again to judge the world.
* All men must repent, receive forgiveness and baptism, and are promised the gift of salvation.[2]

As a teenager, I well remember the preacher holding up five fingers and indicating the New Testament expectation when the gospel has been proclaimed: faith, repentance, confession, baptism and reception of the gift of the Holy Spirit. In recent decades, following the theology of Rudolf Bultmann, a group of European scholars has claimed it is not a series of actions (gospel proclamations) that creates faith in the hearer; rather it is personal encounter with Jesus Christ as Lord which creates faith, which then is demonstrated in personal response.

But true preaching is never static or abstract, but always involves encounter with the living God. When the early Christians preached, faith resulted and the gospel spread. This was in fulfilment of the following command of Christ:

When the Holy Spirit comes upon you, you will be filled with power, and you will be witnesses for me in Jerusalem in all of Judea and Samaria, and to the ends of the earth.[3]

With the spread of this message, a new community came into being. They were known simply as the 'people of the Way'. They were the fellowship of the new age, a community of believers who followed the life and teachings of Jesus, receiving from him the gift of forgiveness and eternal life. What they possessed primarily was not a new creed of doctrine or code of behaviour, but the experience of the indwelling of Jesus.

J.B. Phillips once said:

The great difference between present-day Christianity and that of which we read in these letters is that to us it is primarily a performance, to them it was a real experience. We are apt to reduce the Christian religion to a code, or at best a rule of heart and life. To these men it is quite plainly the invasion of their lives by a new quality of life altogether. They did not hesitate to describe this as Christ 'living in' them.[4]

That newborn church, with all of its freshness and vitality, brought into history a unique and unconquerable spirit. No wonder that others became threatened by their presence and fearful of their message. The Jewish religious leaders (wrongly) accused Stephen of speaking against the Temple and the law of Moses:

We heard him say that this Jesus of Nazareth will tear down the Temple and change all the customs that have come down to us.[5]

The fear that everything would be changed — including their positions of power and status — caused opposition to the young church as much as any profound theological objections. The establishment dragged Christians before the city authorities, shouting: 'These men have caused trouble everywhere!'[6] It was an accusation that was repeated many times.

Opposition to the Christians

The early church faced immense opposition from every sector of society. The growing unrest rapidly spread throughout the whole of Israel.

The *Pharisees*, who had proved so obstinate and confrontationist with Jesus, continued their opposition to the new church. They had very few theological objections — after all, the early Christians carried out many of the traditions of worship approved of by the Pharisees. They attended the Temple not only on every sabbath but every day; they observed the Law. However, those young Christians also kept proclaiming the truth that Jesus was the Messiah. This was too much for the Pharisees. Having had Jesus executed, they now sought to stamp out this new and dangerous teaching. Some of the Pharisees were moved by the courage and witness of the early Christians, subsequently being baptised and joining the believers. Other Pharisees argued strongly that the Christian faith must obey all the commands of Judaism and remain within the fold. Some of these later were to strongly oppose the introduction of Gentiles into the church.

The *Sadducees* violently opposed the Christians who emphasised strongly that God had raised Jesus from the dead. The Sadducees did not believe in the resurrection. Consequently, arguments that Jesus had been raised by God from the dead cut across the very basis of their teaching:

Some Sadducees arrived. They were annoyed because Peter and John were teaching the people that Jesus had risen from death, which proved that the dead will rise to life. So they arrested them and put them in gaol until the next day since it was already late, but many who heard the message believed; and the number of men grew to about five thousand.[7]

Those same Sadducees were to be in the forefront of the movement to have Peter and John also put to death.

Ruins at Qumran where the
Essene Community lived

The *Essenes* were a third group
who played an important part in
the life of ancient Israel. From the
discoveries of the Dead Sea
Scrolls at Qumran, there are some
suggestions that the Essenes were
warmly disposed towards the
young church. It is possible that
John the Baptist had come from
the Essene Community: his
message of repentance and
baptism was very similar to that
of the Essenes; he preached at the
mouth of the river Jordan (one
day's walk from Qumran) and a
number of passages of scripture
used in John's preaching were
favourite verses with the teachers
and writers of the Dead Sea
Scrolls. Today, permanently
enshrined in the Shrine of the
Book in Jerusalem, is the perfectly
preserved copy of the Book of
Isaiah, possibly handled by John
the Baptist.[8]

The early Christians met with
great success as they preached
that Jesus was Lord. Both
ordinary people and even a
number of priests accepted the
faith. Beginning with Old
Testament prophecy (from Moses,
Samuel, Abraham or Joel), they
demonstrated these events were
fulfilled in the life, death and
resurrection of Jesus. Psalm
118:22 was a particularly
favourite passage of scripture
because it indicated that God's
living stone was rejected by the
builders (the Jewish religious
leaders). Jesus the enthroned
Christ, the Son of David, the
promised Messiah, the abused
servant was the rejected corner
stone.

Still the establishment did

succeed in harassing the young church. Its members were persecuted and gaoled. Two of its leaders, Peter and John, were forbidden ever again 'to speak to anyone in the name of Jesus'. However, the young Christians with courage and boldness answered:

You yourselves judge which is right in God's sight — to obey you or to obey God. For we cannot stop speaking of what we ourselves have seen and heard.[9]

They were again later arrested and put in the public gaol. Paul's own teacher, Gamaliel, advocated a cautious response to this new-found teaching. The Sanhedrin agreed:

They called the apostles in, had them whipped, and ordered them never again to speak in the name of Jesus; and then they set them free. As the apostles left the Council, they were happy, because God had considered them worthy to suffer disgrace for the sake of Jesus. And every day in the Temple and in people's homes they continued to teach and preach the good news about Jesus the Messiah.[10]

Obviously, something more had to be done to silence the boldness of the early preachers.

The martyrdom of Stephen
The situation came to a head with the effective preaching of Stephen. He was one of the first deacons, elected by the church to help care for the needy and the poor, distributing money among the widows and the impoverished. A man 'full of faith and the Holy Spirit', Stephen was opposed by a large number of orthodox Jews. Some who were from overseas synagogues debated and argued violently against him. Stephen faced a savage retribution on some trumped-up charges from people who had been bribed. 'We heard him say that this Jesus of Nazareth will tear down the Temple and change all the customs that have come down to us from Moses!'[11]

It is easy to understand how they misconstrued the teaching of Jesus about the Temple, but it was the threat of changing the *customs* more than anything else that caused the religious leaders to move with violence against him.
(a) Stephen's speech
Luke records the speech in which Stephen rehearsed the details of the history of Israel. This was probably a carefully constructed sermon used over and over again by many of the early Christian preachers.

His carefully reasoned, powerfully argued case for Jesus as the fulfilment of the messianic prophecies brought strong reaction from the members of the council. Not only was Stephen blaspheming against the Temple (a charge that was made against Jesus[12]); he was claiming that Jesus had ascended into heaven and was standing in the place of honour and authority beside God.

That was the worst of blasphemies and for that there was a penalty ascribed in the Law:

Take that man out of the camp. Everyone who heard him curse shall put his hands on the man's head to testify that he is guilty, and then the whole community shall stone him to death.[13]

(b) Stephen's stoning
When the Romans conquered Israel, they removed the right of execution of people from the hands of the Jewish Council and put it in the hands of the Roman governor. However, they did allow the Jews one exception to this rule. If anyone should desecrate the sanctity of the Temple in Jerusalem, then the Jews had the authority to execute the man under their own law by their own hands. It was under this provision that Stephen was immediately executed.

Most Sunday School drawings of the stoning of Stephen have completely missed the point. It wasn't a case of a man being surrounded by people who threw stones at him. Death by stoning was much more certain than that. The victim was forced to stand naked on the city wall while the charge against him was read out. He was then thrown down from the wall — perhaps twenty or thirty feet — to the rocks below. His accusers then one at a time would carry boulders to the edge of the wall and drop them down upon his prostrate body.

In one of those touches which authenticate the story, Luke records the witnesses 'left their cloaks in the care of a young man named Saul . . . and Saul approved of his murder.'[14] So Saul of Tarsus is introduced into the history of the Christian church.

The death of Stephen finally succeeded in scattering the believers. Widespread persecution broke out and many of the faithful fled to safer towns, even those in countries outside of Israel:

That very day the church in Jerusalem began to suffer cruel persecution. All of the believers, except the apostles, were scattered throughout the provinces of Judea and Samaria . . . but Saul tried to destroy the church; going from house to house, he dragged out the believers, both men and women, and threw them into gaol.[15]

Later, when Paul was himself on trial for his faith, he described his motives at the time as follows:

I myself thought that I should do everything I could against the cause of Jesus of Nazareth. That is what I did in Jerusalem. I received authority from the chief priests and put many of God's people in prison; and when they were sentenced to death, I also voted against them. Many times I had them punished in the synagogues and tried to make them deny their faith. I was so furious with them that I even went to foreign cities to persecute them.[16]

(c) Stephen's significance
Stephen's death, however, played an important part in the conversion of Saul. The great psychiatrist, Carl Jung, said it was at this point that Saul was actually converted; his later

Damascus road experience was his final surrender to God. Stephen's death started a chain of thoughts in the mind of Saul of Tarsus which must have created a whirlwind of conflicting concepts. Saul's decision to go to Damascus was in response to the rapid spread of the faith.

In his history, Luke carefully records the next stage of the church's outward growth when, like ripples on the surface of a still pond, the influence of the early Christians radiated out into the known world.

Jesus had commanded his disciples to take the message into all the world. The disciples spread the message throughout Jerusalem and Judea. Philip took the message to Samaria. He was supported by Peter and John who helped the word spread in that region. Philip then took the word to the Gaza Strip and the conversion of an Ethiopian then took the message down into the North of Africa. At the same time other Christians were fleeing north into Syria and to Damascus.

Josephus records that there was a large group of Jews in Damascus at this time (AD 35). He mentions that some 18,000 Jewish soldiers from Damascus had died during the Jewish wars. It seems natural that the early Christians would flee for safety to such a large city where many would have relatives and friends who would shelter them. But Saul was a persistent persecutor. Hearing of their presence in Damascus he gained letters of authority in order that he might persecute those who were adulterating the faith, describing it later as his being 'so zealous that I persecuted the church.'[17] The journey with his retinue of soldiers, Temple police and attendants probably took about six days up the hard and hot road into Syria.

Paul, the new man

In all of literature there is probably no more clear account of a person's changed attitude than that of the account repeated several times in the book of Acts on the conversion of Saul. The facts are simple: as he was travelling and approaching Damascus, 'suddenly a light from the sky flashed around him. He fell to the ground and heard a voice saying to him, "Saul, Saul! Why do you persecute me?" "Who are you, Lord?" he asked. "I am Jesus whom you persecute," the voice said. "But get up and go into the city, where you will be told what you must do." '18

Saul saw the light in more ways than one. Later he would write to the Christians in Corinth that 'it is not ourselves that we preach; we preach Jesus Christ as Lord, and ourselves as your servants for Jesus' sake. The God who said, "Out of darkness the light shall shine!" is the same God who made his light shine in our hearts, to bring us the knowledge of God's glory shining in the face of Christ.'19

With the light came a voice asking why he was hurting himself by kicking against the inevitable pressure of God. Saul realised that Jesus Christ was risen from the dead, that he was God's Son and that it was as if Saul was running his hand against the grain of the universe. Everything he had previously said and done had been wrong. The inward illumination was to change Saul's life completely, so much so that from now on he would no longer be known as Saul, but Paul. The change of name indicated to Saul that he now had a task to take the message to his own people

and then beyond them to the Gentiles. Later Paul was to write, 'God in his grace chose me even before I was born, and called me to serve him.'20

What a change was observed outwardly in Paul's life! He came riding in pride and zealousness to persecute the Christians, but now he needed to be helped from the ground and guided, for his eyes had been blinded by the light, and quietly and humbly was led into Damascus where for three days he was unable to see, eat or drink.

Paul's life had been absolutely shattered, but out of that shattering a new man was to emerge. Jesus Christ held him in his grip and his brokenness was simply in order to allow for a new vitality.

Into his life came an older Christian who in the most beautiful way accepted him and helped him to realise what God was doing for him. Ananias heard from the Lord that he should go to the house of Judas in Straight Street where Saul would be praying, lay hands on him, and restore to Saul his sight. Naturally he protested for he knew the reputation of Saul and believed it was a trick in order to capture other Christians. But the Lord said to Ananias, 'I have chosen him to serve me, to make my name known to the Gentiles and kings and to the people of Israel. And I myself will show him all that he must suffer for my sake.'21

In one of the most moving scenes in the New Testament Ananias reaches out to the persecutor and says, 'Brother Saul ... the Lord has sent me — Jesus himself, who appeared to you on the road as you were coming here. He sent me so that you might see again and be filled with the Holy Spirit',[22] giving to Saul the reassurance, comfort and companionship he needed if he was to come within the ranks of those whom he had so bitterly distressed.

Saul's sight returned. He was baptised. He was strengthened by God and immediately went straight to the synagogues and began to preach that Jesus was the Son of God. All who heard him were amazed and asked, 'Isn't he the one who in Jerusalem was killing those who worshipped that man Jesus? And didn't he come here for the very purpose of arresting those people and taking them back to the chief priests?' But Saul's preaching became even more powerful, and his proofs that Jesus was the Messiah were so convincing that the Jews who lived in Damascus could not answer him. The powerful prosecutor had now become an even more powerful advocate for the faith. The old Saul had died and a new Paul was born. His mind, conscience, emotions, will, personality and purpose were all changed. He was literally 'born anew'. So great was the change that later he was called by the new name, Paul.

From his own experience he knew that 'when anyone is joined to Christ, he is a new being; the old is gone and the new has come. All this is done by God, who through Christ changed us from enemies into his friends and gave us the task of making others his friends also. Our message is that God was making all mankind his friends through Christ.'[23] His conversion is the clue to understanding his theology, the power of his ministry, and the force within his life.

This raises some relevant questions:

(a) Did Paul know Jesus?
Paul raises the matter himself when he asks the cryptic questions 'Am I not a free man? Am I not an apostle? Haven't I seen Jesus our Lord?',[24] and, at the end of his list of witnesses of the resurrected Christ: 'Last of all he appeared also to me'.[25] Were these two references to his meeting with Jesus referring to the experience on the Damascus road only?

Paul seems to have considerable evidence about the life and teachings of Jesus. He develops the teachings and spirit of Jesus as no other apostle did. Was this solely as a result of the enquiries that he made after his conversion of the apostle Peter? Paul says, 'It was three years [after I returned to Damascus] that I went to Jerusalem to obtain information from Peter and stayed with him for two weeks. I did not see any other apostle except James, the Lord's brother'.[26]

It was fashionable once to indicate there was a vast difference between the simple Jesus of Galilee in the Gospels and the complex Saviour of the world presented by Paul. However, surely no scholar would today make those same claims: from the epistles of Paul one can gain considerable information about the life of Jesus.

A.M. Hunter lists all the significant factors about the earthly life of Jesus and the insights into the character of Jesus gained through the writings of Paul. The list is long and significant. He also lists the teachings of Jesus alluded to in the writings of Paul and this constitutes a major listing of Christian doctrines. These details of his life, character and teachings indicate a detailed knowledge of the Saviour by Paul.[27]

Paul also gives us further insights into the teachings of Jesus which are not found in any of the Gospels. Further, there are insights taken from the teachings of Jesus that Paul referred to and mentioned in his epistles before the Gospels were ever written, including the way Jesus uses the word 'Abba', Father. In writing to the Corinthians about the question of remarriage he indicates that his guidelines on marriage, divorce, separation and remarriage come not from himself, but from Jesus. In this section Paul goes further than what is revealed in the teachings of Jesus in the Gospels.

In the same way he speaks about the second advent of the Lord to the Thessalonians and presents to us material not found elsewhere in the scriptures. Paul knew Jesus after his conversion in the same way the disciples did when they met with him and talked about his death.

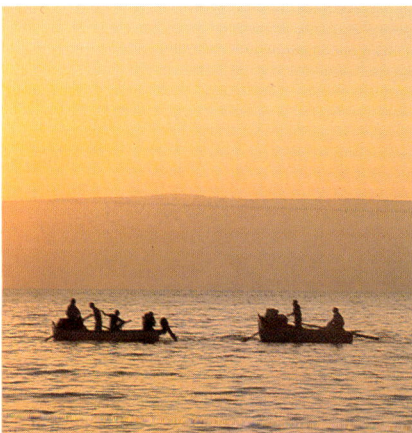

(b) How did Paul learn the teachings of Jesus?

Paul may have learnt much in his brief encounters with Peter and James or, alternatively, by further direct revelation of Christ himself. Only in these ways could he have written of the teachings of Jesus as expressed in the Gospels before they were written.

A careful examination of the parables of Jesus and the teachings of Paul on the question of salvation, the kingdom of God and our redemption show remarkable insights. The dates of his own training in Palestine coincided with the silent years of Jesus prior to his baptism. During the public ministry of Jesus, Paul was back in Tarsus. It seems to me that it was a post-resurrection appearance of Jesus which gave the apostle the insights he needed as he developed the teachings of Jesus through his addresses and letters.

(c) What is the ministry of the Holy Spirit?

From the presence of the Holy Spirit in the first chapter of Acts every new movement within the early church was seen as a direct result of the influence of the Holy Spirit. Jesus had promised that the Spirit would come as a counsellor and companion and would come upon those who believed in him. From the day of Pentecost we see the ministry of the Spirit of God among the leaders of the church. First Peter, then John, then Stephen, then Philip, and now the Spirit is moving through the life of Paul. In a very real sense *The Acts of the Apostles* could be called *The Acts of the Holy Spirit*.

A pattern of conversion

Paul's great turnaround became the pattern of conversion of many Christians over the centuries who have seen in his turnaround the characteristics that they experienced. It was the sensualist *Augustine* who was turned around to become a saint and the greatest mind for the next thousand years, whose life was completely changed through reading some of the writings of Paul. *Martin Luther*, the strong-minded German monk who was anxious about his own salvation, discovered the freedom and grace of God through Paul's Epistle to the Romans. *John Wesley* wrote in his diary on 24 May, 1738: 'about a quarter before nine, while the reader of Luther's preface to the Epistle of Romans was describing the change which God works in the heart through faith in Christ, I felt my heart strangely warmed. I felt I did trust in Christ, Christ alone for my salvation; and an assurance was given to me that he had taken away my sins, even mine, and saved me from the law of sin and death.'

So the roll call has continued into the twentieth century with remarkable conversions, all of which have revealed some of the same characteristics as that of the apostle Paul. *Chuck Colson*, known as 'the hatchet man' for President Nixon, who was imprisoned for his involvement in the American Watergate scandal, found himself transformed from one of the most powerful men in the American White House to a prisoner in a dark cell. It was there he said he recalled Paul's words to the Romans: 'Do not be conformed to this world, but be transformed by the renewal of your mind, that you may prove what is the will of God, that which is good and acceptable and perfect'. (Romans 12:2). 'The more I mused on it,' said Colson, 'the more I realised what a key verse of scripture it is — maybe *the* key verse for growing up as a Christian. Grasping this concept was a turning point for me, as it is, I suspect, for many Christians. God, I now understood, was working a powerful transformation in my thought habits and forcing me to think about what it really means to live as a disciple of Christ.'[28]

At the other end of the social strata, far from the White House with its trappings of power and wealth, an impoverished black, *John Perkins*, attended an adult Sunday School in Pasadena and studied the life of the apostle Paul. 'How could religion mean so much to anybody like Paul? The question hounded me all summer. The answer came as I grappled with Paul's message of law and grace. Paul wrote: "I am crucified with Christ: nevertheless I live, yet not I, but Christ liveth in me, and the life which I now live in the flesh I live by faith in the Son of God who loved me, and gave himself for me" (Galatians 2:20). At the age of twenty-seven for the first time in my life I came to see that the Christian life was more than what I was seeing in the churches. It was the outliving of the inliving Christ. I knew Christ wasn't living inside me. I felt a deep hunger to know him in this personal way.'[29] So began the turnaround in an uneducated, poor negro's life which was in turn to lead him through education, status, position on presidential commissions and leadership among twentieth century blacks.

The quest for the conversion experience continues in the lives of many people. But it is not an experience that can be achieved or manufactured. The conversion experience is the outworking of the inner revealing of the resurrected Jesus. It was the belief in Christ as Lord and Saviour that more than anything explains the phenomenal influence on the world that was Paul. The English poet, John Betjeman, said:

> St Paul is often criticised
> By modern people who're annoyed
> At his conversion, saying Freud
> Explains it all. But they omit
> The really vital point of it,
> Which isn't **how** it was achieved
> But what it was that Paul believed.[30]

God had touched him, turned him round, transformed his life, and now had thrust him into his service. Ananias had been used by God in the healing of Paul's blindness, in his baptism and in his encouragement to Paul as he commenced preaching immediately to the believers and to the Jews in the synagogues.

So powerful was Paul's presentation and personal change in life that some of his former companions decided that he must be silenced. A plot was hatched to kill him. 'But he was told of their plan. Day and night they watched the city gates in order to kill him. But one night Saul's followers took him and let him down through an opening in the wall, lowering him in a basket.'[31]

A desert experience

Paul tells us that he went into the Nabataean kingdom in the area of Arabia where he spent time in prayer and study. He was in the area of Mount Horeb where both Moses and Elijah had communed with God in previous generations. He spent time reflecting on his conversion, on the reality of the resurrected Jesus and on his understanding of what Jesus was accomplishing through his life, death and resurrection. Paul claimed that his gospel came to him 'by revelation' and it was probably during this desert experience that he grew in his understanding of his faith and allegiance to Christ. It was here that he probably also witnessed to the caravans of people that travelled through the desert area.

The desert experience was an essential part of the spiritual growth of Moses, Elijah, Amos, John the Baptist and even Jesus. For Paul it was a time of sorting out his turned-around attitudes, of reflection on his persecution of the followers of Jesus, of dialogue with his Lord, and re-shaping of his life by Jesus.

Paul's subsequent years were not easy. He went to Jerusalem to try to join the disciples but they would not accept him or believe that he was a disciple out of their fear of him. Paul came to Jerusalem and made contact with the apostles, speaking with Peter and James over a two-week period. Paul was proud of the fact that by that time he had already learnt much of the Christian faith and that it had not been necessary for him to 'confer with flesh and blood'. However, he was undoubtedly at this time confirmed by Peter in his understanding and directions. How we want to know the background! 'It was three years later that I went to Jerusalem to obtain information from Peter.'[32] What was this information he obtained? Luke indicates that it was through Barnabas that Paul was brought together with Peter and James while the other disciples were not yet willing to accept him. Such an intermediary role would have been quite typical of Barnabas and explains how later Barnabas knew exactly the sort of man he was after when he went and searched for Paul to help him in the fulfilment of the missionary command of God.

Bold speaking
Paul's boldness in proclaiming Jesus and his capacity to dispute and argue through the necessity of the cross and the resurrection resulted in a number of Greek-speaking Jews wanting to kill him. Already early in his career Paul was discovering what the penalty of bold proclamation was for the earnest disciple. After his brief reappearance in Jerusalem he was, for the second time in his life as a Christian, smuggled out of the city, being taken this time to Caesarea and from there on to Tarsus.[33]

The immediate impact of Saul's conversion, according to Luke, is that 'the church throughout Judea, Galilee and Samaria had a time of peace. Through the help of the Holy Spirit it was strengthened and grew in numbers, as it lived in reverence for the Lord.'[34] The church by now had grown not only through Jerusalem, Judea, Galilee and Samaria, but was also developing in Syria and, with the return of Paul to Tarsus, in Cilicia.

Paul spent the next years of his life in Tarsus and in the area surrounding his home town still preaching the faith he had once tried to destroy. He travelled throughout places in Syria and Cilicia proclaiming the truth and many came to faith because of his witness.

Paul had a commitment to the law of Moses in his early life that led him even to persecute the church. Now he had a commitment to Jesus that was to lead him to take the gospel throughout the entire empire.

His obligation to proclaim the gospel started with his complete turnaround in his conversion on the road to Damascus. It was only to end in Rome at the point of his execution.

For personal reading

Theme: Persecutor transformed

MONDAY — Filled with the Spirit
Acts 2:1-21

TUESDAY — Repent and be baptised
Acts 2:29-42

WEDNESDAY — Compelled to witness
Acts 4:13-22

THURSDAY — A forgiving spirit
Acts 7:51-60

FRIDAY — Touched by Christ
Acts 26:9-18

SATURDAY — Anointed for service
Acts 9:10-19

SUNDAY — Strengthened by the Lord
Acts 9:19-31

For group study

Topic: Resurrection power and new life

1 Discuss the difference between Christianity as a 'religious code' and the Christian faith as a 'personal experience' of the risen Lord.

2 What do you understand by the term 'Messiah'? How did Jesus fufil the role of the Messiah?

3 Can you tell the story of Paul's conversion on the road to Damascus in your own words?

4 In what way did Paul 'know' Jesus and his teachings?

5 Have you also had a conversion experience? What was it that caused you to turn around from sin to salvation?

6 What were some of the proofs of Paul's conversion and growth in faith?

3

Paul the Preacher

To discover who you are is to make the most profound discovery of all. Then to be what you say you are is the greatest challenge of all.

Following his conversion on the Damascus road, Paul set out to become what he said he was. His life had meaning, integration and purpose. In discovering Jesus, Paul discovered himself.

On the Damascus road Paul came to himself. The prodigal son came to himself in a pig pen. Any place and any time can be the place and time when God becomes real in our lives and we see the light, and so come to ourselves.

After his conversion Paul immediately became a preacher of the gospel. He was to spend the rest of his life proclaiming the good news.

Where Paul preached

Paul's preaching was done in four basic locations: in private homes, in Jewish synagogues, in public halls and in the open air.

1. Private homes

The home was the fundamental unit of society within the Roman, Greek and Jewish worlds. It had the wonderful advantage of being a small intimate group of people which allowed for questioning and discussion to take place. Paul used to be invited to the homes of people in the areas to which he travelled, entering their home for hospitality, and being led into discussions about the faith.

An early occasion where this took place was when Peter stopped at the house of Simon the Tanner at Joppa and from there went to the house of Cornelius in Caesarea. In both places people came to faith which resulted in baptisms and receiving the gift of the Holy Spirit.

Paul frequently stayed during his travels at the homes of Jews who were interested in the Messianic promises and who became Christians, or in the homes of Gentiles who feared God and became the basis of a church in their areas. So in Thessalonica, Jason's house became the centre of a new church in that area; and in

Corinth right opposite the synagogue where Paul had had some dispute was the home of Titius Justus and there Paul established a teaching ministry which led to the church in Corinth.

It is not surprising that preaching in houses became the first means by which the early church grew. Jesus was a frequent guest in the home of Simon Peter's mother-in-law at Capernaum, frequently stayed in the home of Mary, Martha and Lazarus at Bethany, and probably held the Passover meal in the home of John Mark's mother in Jerusalem. Very soon this particular house passed into history, being known as the home with the upper room in which the Last Supper was held and the early church gathered for prayer, and in which the disciples received the Holy Spirit.

An interesting example of a household meeting, albeit a very large house, is found in the account of a Saturday evening during Paul's last visit to Troas After they had shared in a fellowship meal or Communion, we read:

Paul spoke to the people and kept on speaking until midnight, since he was going to leave the next day. Many lamps were burning in the upstairs room where we were meeting. A young man named Eutychus was sitting in the window, and as Paul kept on talking, Eutychus got sleepier and sleepier, until he finally went sound asleep and fell from the third storey to the ground. When they picked him up, he was dead. But Paul went down and threw himself on him and hugged him. 'Don't worry,' he said. 'He is still alive!' Then he went back upstairs, broke bread, and ate. After talking with them for a long time, even until sunrise, Paul left. They took the young man home alive and were greatly comforted.[1]

Paul took every opportunity to preach the good news about Jesus and, speaking in home meetings, he established churches. The phrase 'the church that meets in your house' became a common usage in the early church. Twenty centuries later it is interesting to see the rise once more of the house church, and just as Christians met in the house of Philemon which formed the nucleus of a group of believers, so today house churches are established in every continent of the earth, being the forerunner of a more formal larger congregation covering an area. Some very large churches with tens of thousands of members, and some super-churches with hundreds of thousands of members, base their growth and existence on one central mother church building, surrounded by hundreds and even tens of thousands of smaller local house churches where the host is the pastor and teacher for the small group of believers who gather in their house for prayer, fellowship, teaching and the celebration of communion.

2. Jewish synagogues
Immediately after his conversion and the sharing of his faith with the other believers under the leadership of Ananias, Paul 'went straight to the synagogues and began to preach that Jesus was the son of God'.[2] His recorded speeches in synagogues all follow a similar pattern. Although the house group provided

opportunities for dialogue, for question and answer and perhaps debate, the synagogues provided a more formal environment where any visiting teacher, and especially a visiting Pharisee, was invited to read the scriptures and to teach from them. As Paul travelled he went first to the synagogues where he was given the opportunity of opening the scriptures and his pattern of preaching follows a similar line.

The fullest report of his preaching in a synagogue is found in Antioch in Pisidia. 'On the Sabbath they went into the synagogue and sat down. After the reading from the Law of Moses and from the writings of the prophets, the officials of the synagogue sent them a message: "Brothers, we want you to speak to the people if you have a message of encouragement for them." Paul stood up, motioned with his hand, and began to speak.'[3] His speech in the synagogues was a carefully constructed sermon. After graciously greeting his hosts, Paul recited the history of the Jewish people indicating how God had chosen and made them a great nation, how the people loved the traditions of their forefathers, how they triumphed over great difficulties and something of their expectation of the coming of the Messiah.

His second point was that Jesus of Nazareth was the fulfilment of the expectations of a Messiah, the one promised by John the Baptist to bring salvation. Paul said that it was people who lived in Jerusalem who had taken Jesus, the one spoken about by the prophets, passed the death sentence on him and asked Pilate to have him put to death. But after his death and burial, God raised him from the dead as a sign that he was the Messiah. Paul quoted from the prophets and from the psalms to prove that Jesus was not only the long-prophesied Messiah but the very rationale for their existence as a nation.

Like any good preacher, Paul hammered home his message. 'All of you, my fellow Israelites, are to know for sure that it is through Jesus that the message about forgiveness of sins is preached to you; you are to know that everyone who believes in him is set free from all the sins from which the Law of Moses could not set you free' and he finally warned them to take seriously God's mercy lest they scoff at the message and be rejected.

This sermon was typical of the message that Paul gave to Jews in the synagogue. It is interesting to note that after he had finished the sermon the people invited him to come back the next Sabbath and tell them more about these things and that a number of the people, including both Jews and Gentiles, followed them home and discussed the matter further with them in private.[3]

Paul, like any good preacher, started where they were, understanding their pride in their history and their knowledge of the scriptures. He took them through their own history leading up to the central place occupied by Jesus Christ. He respected their dignity and knowledge of the scriptures, but courageously and pointedly indicated that Jesus was the answer to their deepest needs and required belief and commitment.

3. Public halls

When Paul took the message of Jesus Christ throughout Turkey, Macedonia and Greece, he found many public places in which he could proclaim the gospel. The Greeks were used to public teachers and had many lyceums, or public halls, for teaching and philosophical debate available for visiting lecturers. A public hall had the advantage of providing a reliable venue to teach consistently over a period of time people who would be willing to come and hear him at a regular hour, and was less likely to attract the attention of hooligans and the public police who on a number of occasions broke up Paul's open-air meetings.

A classic example of him preaching in a public hall occurred in Ephesus on his second visit. He had returned to this centre to strengthen 'all the believers' and for the first three months went into the synagogues and proclaimed his usual gospel message, speaking 'boldly with the people' and 'trying to convince them about the kingdom of God.'

After he had been rejected by a number of the more conservative Jews in the synagogue, 'Paul left them and took the believers with him, and every day from 11 a.m. to 4 p.m. he held discussions in the lecture hall of Tyrannus. This went on for two years, so that all the people who lived in the province of Asia, both Jews and Gentiles, heard the word of the Lord.' Apparently the lecturer Tyrannus — not a very flattering name for any teacher! — only held classes in the early morning and in the later afternoon and Paul hired the lecture hall during the middle of the day, probably spending the rest of his time earning his living.[4]

The Celsus Library: Ephesus

View of Athens from the Propylaia

Unfortunately we do not have an example of Paul's lectures in public. However, judging from his other speeches before both Jews and Gentiles we believe that they would have followed a similar pattern, being relevant to his hearers, quoting local authorities and poets, emphasising the fulfilment of the scriptures in Jesus, and of God's special work of salvation through the man Jesus who was rejected, crucified, buried, but whom God raised from the dead and expects people to believe in for the forgiveness of their sins.

4. The open air
Different generations have found the value of open-air preaching: Lord Soper in recent years spoke to hundreds of people daily on Tower Hill, London; John Wesley and George Whitefield addressed tens of thousands at open air meetings; Jesus gave his greatest teachings on the mountainside, on the level plains, and along the seashore.

Peter preached in the open air on the day of Pentecost, and the early disciples took the message about Jesus into the market places, along the lakes and river banks, in the open fields, and in the town squares. Paul frequently preached in the open, debating with hecklers and ruffians as the case required. Frequently there was great danger to the speaker from flying stones and public assaults.

In Athens Paul had a marvellous opportunity in the most famous public arena of all to proclaim the eternal truths. With the Areopagus and the Acropolis as a breathtaking backdrop, Paul stood in the open Agora and began speaking to any who would listen.

Having commenced with an illustration that they all knew and understood, Paul moved quickly to explain to them the God they did not know. He stressed God's greatness and creative power, quoted from some of their own contemporary authors, outlined his own theology of God and made God's commands clear. He immediately led to Jesus and his resurrection at which point he was interrupted.[5]

This initial address in the open air had a remarkable impact in view of the fact that these people of Athens were used to hearing philosophers and debaters. It is interesting to note that in Athens today the names of the philosophers and debaters are completely unknown, and the only names that survive from this era are the names of those who believed in Jesus because of Paul's preaching in the open.

So Paul the preacher took every opportunity to proclaim how God worked in history through the nation Israel, through the prophets who foretold the coming of the Messiah, and through Jesus of Nazareth who was both Lord and Christ.

He took the opportunity in private homes, in Jewish synagogues, in public halls and in the open air to proclaim his message. Throughout his life, Paul lived true to himself, a preacher of the gospel:

So then, where does that leave the wise, or the scholars, or the skilful debaters of this world? God has shown that this world's wisdom is foolishness! For God in his wisdom made it impossible for people to know him by means of their own wisdom. Instead, by means of the so-called "foolish" message we preach, God decided to save those who believe. Jews want miracles for proof, and Greeks look for wisdom. As for us, we proclaim the crucified Christ, a message that is offensive to the Jews and nonsense to the Gentiles; but for those whom God has called, both Jews and Gentiles, this message is Christ, who is the power of God and the wisdom of God. [6]

What are the main themes in the recorded sermons of Paul? The best of Paul's theology can be seen in his letters to the church at Ephesus and to the church at Rome. Indeed his clearest and finest doctrinal summary is in the first eight chapters of Romans. This is the closest Paul ever comes to a carefully reasoned, sustained, theological presentation.

However, a study of Paul's addresses and sermons in *The Acts of the Apostles* provides the key theological insights to Paul's preaching.

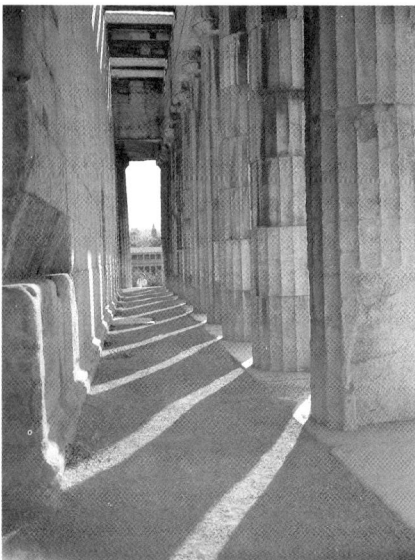

The preaching themes of Paul

Although many themes in his preaching can be named, there are six that are constantly presented.

1. The righteousness of God

It is Paul's understanding of the nature and character of God that becomes the basis of his preaching. 'Salvation is of the Lord'. That became the basis of all that Paul preached. Salvation is from and of God and in the good news the righteousness of God is revealed: 'I have complete confidence in the gospel; it is God's power to save all who believe, first the Jews and also the Gentiles. For the gospel reveals how God puts people right with himself: it is through faith from beginning to end. As the scripture says, "The person who is put right with God through faith shall live".'[7]

Salvation does not depend upon man's moral or ethical achievements but solely upon God's grace and mercy. Our salvation is not earned or purchased or achieved by anything that we do. 'It is by God's grace that you have been saved through faith. It is not the result of your own efforts, but God's gift, so that no one can boast about it.'[8]

With our reception of God's righteousness, we receive peace, joy and the hope of glory. This *being put right with God* is at the heart of our salvation. No matter how much humans might sin, God's grace is such that it expands and covers even the greatest of sins. 'Where sin increased, God's grace increased much more. So then, just as sin ruled by means of death, so also God's grace rules by means of righteousness, leading us to

eternal life through Jesus Christ our Lord.'[9]

The key to our relationship with God is *being put right* with God and that is appropriated by us through God's own grace and mercy.

2. The sinfulness of man

Each one of us is less than we ought to be. Like Humpty Dumpty, all of us have had a great fall, and not all the king's horses and all the king's men can put us together again! Every psychiatrist has patients who tell him that the patient is not what he ought to be, and that he is powerless to be different.

Paul out of his own experience speaks of how far each of us is from what we ought to be:

God puts people right through their faith in Jesus Christ. God does this to all who believe in Christ, because there is no difference at all: everyone has sinned and is far away from God's saving presence. But by the free gift of God's grace all are put right with him through Christ Jesus who sets them free. God offered him, so that by his sacrificial death he should become the means by which people's sins are forgiven through their faith in him.[10]

In the mid-1970s we watched the agony of Watergate. One of President Nixon's closest aides, Chuck Colson, watched the President's resignation from prison. Ten years later Chuck Colson reflected: 'Mr Nixon's greatest legacy may not be the oft-neglected good points of his presidency but the flaws of his character. For they remind us that even presidents are human, or sinners, as the Bible puts it so

indelicately.'[11] Before you can
ever get your life together, you
have to realise just how far from
God you are. That is why decent
living people who have no need
for God can be further from God
than the person who has publicly
sinned and is overwhelmed with
guilt. For the guilty one can come
to God but the self-sufficient one
remains lost.

Paul stressed our human nature
and our apartness from God. He
described this as being *in Adam*:
our humanness which we all share
incorporates the sin that Adam
committed. Our common
humanity involves us in an
attitude and tendency towards
self-sufficiency, pride and
independence from God.[12] One of
the common threads entwined
throughout humanity is our
general state of depravity. There
is within the marrow of our bones
the genes of our own destruction.
There is nothing that we can do
about it to put ourselves right
with God. The nature of man is
unrighteousness.

Such is our human predicament.
Anyone who knows anything of
human history, of the way we
misuse every scientific and
technological invention and pervert
the results of science, has no
doubt that man ultimately is his
own greatest enemy and the
results of our unchecked humanity
are disaster, disease and death.

Paul indicates man's moral
bankruptcy in one of the most
terrible passages in the Bible. He
outlines man's immorality,
emptiness and futile living. It
starts with man's basic idolatry
'exchanging' the truth about God
for a lie; they worship and serve
what God has created instead of

the Creator himself. That idolatry
leads to immorality. 'Because they
do this God has given them over
to shameful passions. Even the
women pervert the natural use of
their sex by unnatural acts. In the
same way the men give up natural
sexual relations with women and
burn with passion for each other.
Men do shameful things with each
other, and as a result they bring
upon themselves the punishment
they deserve for the wrongdoing.
Because those people refuse to
keep in mind the true knowledge
about God, he has given them
over to corrupted minds.' Human
depravity leads to personal
conflicts, wickedness, greed, vice,
fightings, murder and every kind
of unpleasant relationship. The
list is miserable. Their only
response is to rationalise what
they are doing. 'They know that
God's law says that people who
live this way deserve death. Yet,
not only do they continue to do
these very things, but they even
approve of others who do them.'[13]

Mankind shares with Adam a
humanity that bears the seeds of
its own destruction. 'But God...'
For Paul those two favourite
words change every scene. 'But
now God's way of putting people
right with himself has been
revealed... God puts people right
through their faith in Jesus Christ.
God does this to all who believe
in Christ.'[14]

In Jesus Christ we have a
second Adam. Just as sin entered
the world through the first Adam,
so forgiveness and life eternal
came through Jesus Christ. God
gave his son as a gift to overcome
the result of the sin of Adam and
with him all mankind since.[15] John
Calvin has said, 'Christ was more

Philippi

powerful to save than Adam to ruin.'[16]

When through our faith we are incorporated into Christ, we take upon ourselves the essential nature of Christ and become a new person. Christians by their faith are incorporated into the life of Christ and appropriate to themselves his qualities and character.

That is as far as we need to go for our eternal salvation no matter how apart from God we have been. However, so rich is his character that we still have a long way to grow in Christian maturity. We need to grow in grace and in character to become more like Christ. 'We shall all come together to that oneness in our faith and in our knowledge of the Son of God; we shall become mature people, reaching to the very height of Christ's full stature.'[17]

In all of Paul's talk about our humanity he stresses our sin, rather than our sins. Today people like to refer to sins rather than sin. It is easy to point to the wrongdoings of others and to indicate that on a scale of preference we are not as bad as some other people. But sins are only the symptoms of sin and it is that sin — our apartness from God — which is the common factor all humanity shares. Because of this apartness from God we commit sins according to the influence of our heredity, our environment and our personal response. It is not the sins that distinguish us, it is the fact that we all are in sin by being apart from God. The good news is that God in Christ has overcome our sin and enabled us to belong to the new humanity.

3. Christ — the wisdom and power of God

It was to be expected that the Greeks with their long traditions of philosophy and honouring of wisdom should regard a message of a crucified and resurrected carpenter as being 'foolish' and beneath their intellectual level. Paul would point out that it was that very attitude of intellectual superiority that condemned them.

For what seems to be God's foolishness is wiser than human wisdom, and what seems to be God's weakness is stronger than human strength. Now remember what you were, my brothers, when God called you. From the human point of view few of you were wise or powerful or of high social standing. God purposely chose what the world considers nonsense in order to shame the wise, and he chose what the world considers weak in order to shame the powerful. He chose what the world looks down on and despises and thinks is nothing in order to destroy what the world thinks is important. This means that no one can boast in God's presence. But God has brought you into union with Christ Jesus, and God has made Christ to be our wisdom. By him we are put right with God; we have become God's holy people and are set free.[18]

How God turns upside down the values of the world. God's love in Christ reveals his power to save us and the way he chooses to save us is an example of his understanding of the true nature of people. From the time of our baptism we are to live in the way of Jesus. Jesus Christ has now become the head of a new humanity.

4. The power of the cross

The cross is at the one time a past event, a present experience, and a future encounter. The cross is a *past event* anchored in human history. Salvation has already been accomplished through what Christ did upon the cross. His death, once and for all, ensured the salvation of all who would believe.

Because of our sin we inherit death. Sin finds expression through our flesh, and our humanness is expressed frequently by Paul by the phrase 'in the flesh'. To live after the flesh is to live in sinful self-reliance. Because man seeks to regulate how he should live, laws are given both by man and by God and our humanness results in a legalistic attitude of knowing we are wrong and trying to correct it by living according to laws. By obedience and correct living we hope to gain righteousness. Paul's word was simple: the law is powerless to save us and 'a person becomes an enemy of God when he is controlled by his human nature; for he does not obey God's law and in fact he cannot obey it. Those who obey their human nature cannot please God.'[19]

What God has done upon the cross in Christ Jesus is to make us completely new people. Christ through his self-sacrifice has enabled us, by the appropriation of what he has done through our faith, to be seen as brand-new people. Hence the living Christ is the means by which we are saved.

But the cross is also a *present experience*. Because God has saved us on the cross, we have been freed from sin in order that we might now live a life in conformity to Christ. There is no way that we should continue to live in sin. 'Should we continue to live in sin so that God's grace will increase? Certainly not! We have died to sin — how then can we go on living in it?'[20] Once we have been saved we are committed to serve God through the quality of our living and by the service of our lives.

Paul roundly condemned the thought that any life of good deeds can save us, but he commended the thought that once we are saved we should live a life full of good deeds. Our human effort is no condition of salvation, but is a consequence of it. We have been freed from sin, the law and death so consequently we shall live not as slaves of sin but as slaves of God. 'Surely you know that when you surrender yourselves as slaves to obey someone, you are in fact the slaves of the master you obey — either of sin, which results in death, or of obedience, which results in being put right with God. But thanks be to God! For though at one time you were slaves to sin, you have obeyed with all your heart the truths found in the teaching you received.

You were set free from sin and became the slaves of righteousness.'[21] As a result now we must continue to serve God as his saved people. Our salvation is at the one time a gift from God and a task to be completed. Even when God is living within us we still have to complete our salvation in present experience: 'Keep on working with fear and trembling to complete your salvation, because God is always at work in you to make you willing and able to obey his own purpose.'[22]

The power of the cross is a *future encounter*. Our salvation has been completed upon the cross, yet it is simultaneously lived out in our daily experience and it is yet to be consummated. When we are freed from death and part of his eternal kingdom our salvation will be complete. There is a future consummation that will be found in the complete restoration and renewal of the whole cosmic order. It is not only believing humans that are saved: the entire creation will be renewed and remade. That Christian hope which starts now is complete at the omega point of time. We cannot even comprehend how incredibly beautiful will be that final consummation of all things.

Paul says quite clearly 'we were saved'[23] and 'we are being saved'[24] and 'we will be saved'[25] and all three tenses attributing the power of the cross are used in the one text: 'Now that we have been put right with God through faith, we have peace with God through our Lord Jesus Christ. He has brought us by faith into this experience of God's grace, in which we now live. And so we boast of the hope we have of sharing God's glory.'[26]

5. Salvation for all who have faith

The fifth aspect of Paul's preaching is that salvation is available to everyone who has faith. The old human distinctions are all done away with. Our sex is irrelevant, our socio-economic status is irrelevant, our religious tradition is irrelevant: we are now one in Christ provided we have a common faith in him.

Paul took the message to the Gentiles which indicated that they too could be part of God's family. 'You were apart from Christ. You were foreigners and did not belong to God's chosen people. You had no part in the covenants, which were based upon God's promises to his people, and you lived in this world without hope and without God. But now, in union with Christ Jesus, you, who used to be far away, have been brought near by the sacrificial death of Christ. For Christ himself has brought us peace by making Jews and Gentiles one people...'[27]

Over and over again Paul emphasises that alienation has now been overcome by reconciliation, that condemnation has been annulled by justification, that human guilt has been cleansed by expiation through his blood. Everyone can now be part of God's faithful through faith.

Paul is uncompromising in his declaration that salvation is by faith only: 'for the gospel reveals how God puts people right with himself: it is through faith from beginning to end. As the scripture says, "the person who is put right with God through faith shall live".'[28] It is through faith that we can become God's holy people and be set free.

6. The spirit within

The final aspect of the preaching of Paul is found in his continued emphasis upon God's spirit within the believer.

The Holy Spirit's presence within the believer is central to Christian teaching. The Holy Spirit came upon the believers at the time of Pentecost as evidence of the fulfilment of the prophecy of Joel.[29] It was the Holy Spirit that witnessed that Jesus was the Messiah. The Holy Spirit, Paul explained, is the guarantee or the earnest of God's abiding presence with us. The Holy Spirit is a pledge of our immortality. 'You also became God's people when you heard the true message, the Good News that brought you salvation. You believed in Christ, and God put his stamp of ownership on you by giving you the Holy Spirit he had promised. The Spirit is the guarantee that we shall receive what God has promised his people, and this assures us that God will give complete freedom to those who are his.'[30] The Holy Spirit comes upon us at the time of our baptism and is associated with our response to Christ in faith and our receiving of the forgiveness of sins. The Holy Spirit is the one who brings us together in unity and incorporates us into Christ's body.

These six themes are stressed again and again in the preaching of Paul. He was truly 'occupied with preaching'. Throughout all of his life the apostle used every opportunity to tell out the message outlined here. Preaching with Paul wasn't an occupation; it was his preoccupation.

For personal reading

Theme: Preaching salvation

MONDAY
Sinful nature of man
Romans 3:19-28

TUESDAY
Salvation through faith
Romans 2:8-17

WEDNESDAY
Power in the cross
1 Corinthians 1:10-25

THURSDAY
Man's helpless condition
Romans 1:18-32

FRIDAY
Lord of all
Romans 3:21-26

SATURDAY
Free gift through Christ
Romans 5:12-21

SUNDAY
Jesus breaks all fetters
Romans 6:1-14

For group study

Topic: The preacher of the faith

1 What was the place of house-meetings in the time of Paul? How effective are they today?

2 Is there a style in Paul's preaching? What can we learn from Paul about communicating the truth with other people?

3 How close should the preacher be to his preaching?

4 What is your concept of God and man?

5 How does Paul deal with the question of man's sin?

6 If the cross of Jesus means salvation to Paul, what does it mean to you?

7 How does God's Spirit work in individual lives?

4

Paul the Pastor

The greatest problem facing the parish minister today is that of burn-out. Beneath every minister's name-tag should read the words: 'Caution: Ministry is a health hazard!'

Most ministers committed to God and to the care of the churches pay a high personal price: the cost of caring.

Jesus cared for people. He was the good shepherd, a pastor who cared for them. He laid down his life for his sheep because he loved them. He called Peter three times, 'Do you love me? — Feed my sheep ... Feed my flock ... Tend my lambs.'

Ever since, men and women who have heard the call of Christ have undertaken to be shepherds to the flock of God. They care for his sheep. They are his pastors. The apostle Paul said that in order to help the church, God gave to the church the gifts of apostles, prophets, evangelists, pastors and teachers. These pastor/teachers are the people we see day–by–day caring for the church.[1]

But there is a cost in caring for the church and many faithful ministers burn out in paying that price. In any battle, you can expect heavy casualties among the front line troops. And pastors are in the front line of spiritual battle.

Ever since the beginning faithful men of God have become

overwhelmed and despaired. Elijah, after one of the most successful ministries ever in the name of the Lord, was exhausted and, at the height of his popularity and success, 'walked a whole day into the wilderness. He stopped and sat down in the shade of a tree and wished he would die. "It's too much, Lord," he prayed. "Take away my life; I might as well be dead!" '[2] Jeremiah and Peter had similar experiences. In recent times a number of studies have been made covering hundreds of pastors who have burnt out and left the ministry.

It has been discovered there are a number of similarities among the burn-out casualties. Those leaving the ministry or collapsing within it are usually men in the mid-life age span, who do not have personal care shown to them by the leaders of their denomination at the denominational headquarters; mostly pastoring small congregations; mostly moving frequently from church to church; and mostly with a theology that is at odds with what they were taught in theological college.

It is interesting to note that the apostle Paul had all of those same similarities in his life and ministry.

The causes are also identifiable in the examination of contemporary burn-out victims: some pastors cannot provide the rugged individualism that is required by the ministry with its variety of demands; some find their beautiful idealism shattered by congregations that lapse into old ways and who resist change; some find the financial pressures of a ministry too great and have to take other work to supplement their income; and some lack the support of a spouse who provides constant support in what is a very lonely job.

Again it is interesting to note that the apostle Paul could be identified with each of those causes. Consequently it is interesting to compare the first and the twentieth centuries and to see what it was that enabled Paul to cope with the cost of caring.

Laodicea

Paul and the pressures of pastoring
Recently I took a scoresheet that had been produced to help ministers discover areas of stress in their lives today and then, using that scoresheet, I carefully studied more than half of the New Testament examining both the epistles of Paul and the accounts in Acts about him, paying special attention to his speeches and personal comments in his writing.

I identified a number of pressure points and a similar number of enabling factors.

The pressure points faced by the apostle from his own words and writing are very similar to the causes of burn-out among contemporary ministers.

1. The physical dangers of his work
Paul was both a preacher and a travelling missionary and as a result he was open to all kinds of physical hardship, threat and hurt.

I identified more than thirty occasions in his life, in descriptions of events or in references through his writings, when he was under extreme physical danger. While it is not possible to list them all in detail, the following phrases give a very good picture of the physical danger involved in his work:

The Jews met together and made plans to kill Saul, but he was told of their plan. Day and night they watched the city gates in order to kill him. [3]

He . . . disputed with the Greek-speaking Jews, but they tried to kill him. [4]

Paul was well aware of the dangers he ran and he made frequent reference to those dangers.

He referred to these in his epistles,

particularly when writing to the church at Corinth where he had faced a number of difficult situations. Following an attack upon his life, he reflected upon the dangers that he constantly faced in these words:

'My brothers, I face death every day!' [5]

Paul summed it up in one of the most famous paragraphs of any of his letters:

I have worked much harder, I have been in prison more times, I have been whipped much more, and I have been near death more often. Five times I was given the thirty-nine lashes by the Jews; three times I was whipped by the Romans; and once I was stoned. I have been in three shipwrecks, and once I spent twenty-four hours in the water. In my many travels I have been in danger from floods and from robbers, in danger from fellow Jews and from Gentiles; there have been dangers in the cities, dangers in the wilds, dangers on the high seas, and dangers from false friends. There has been work and toil; often I have gone without sleep; I have been hungry and thirsty; I have often been without enough food, shelter, or clothing. And not to mention other things, every day I am under the pressure of my concern for all the churches. [6]

2. The daily burden of the churches
As a pioneer cross-cultural missionary Paul found even the physical strain of establishing new congregations a great burden. New communities, new languages, new customs, a new tent-making workshop, all must have been a tremendous mental strain. But if you add to this the problems of being rejected, of being physically assaulted and attacked, as well as

the burden of the young Christians who in their eagerness and sometimes wilfulness perverted their new faith, it is easy to appreciate that daily burden of 'the care of all the churches.'

Anybody who has travelled through central Turkey over some of the most rugged mountainous terrain possible would be amazed at the physical stamina that Paul and his companions showed. Yet that was just a small portion of years of constant travelling in some of the most inhospitable countries of the Mediterranean:

Paul and his companions sailed from Paphos and came to Perga, a city in Pamphylia . . . They went on from Perga and arrived in Antioch in Pisidia, and on the Sabbath they went into the synagogue. [7]

Sometimes the joy over a congregation such as at Philippi[8] must have balanced up other congregations where there was constant strain and worry. Constantly the inability of ordinary Christians to maintain a consistent quality of Christian life ate into the very heart of Paul. That daily worry would be enough to turn any man from his calling. Sexual immorality, a spirit of pride and boastfulness, an inability to relate to other people, and the temptation to always turn from the true path of the faith to accommodate the pressures of the world were always the problems the young churches faced and were at the centre of Paul's consistent care. In writing to the Galatians, for example, Paul says: 'I am worried about you! Can it be that all my work for you has been for nothing? . . . My dear children! Once again, just like a

mother in childbirth, I feel the same kind of pain for you until Christ's nature is formed in you. How I wish that I were with you now, so that I could take a different attitude toward you. I am so worried about you!'[9]

3. The pressures of managing the church

Although Paul didn't have a formal religious function, he did have a spiritual oversight over a vast area and a large number of churches, ministers and lay ministers. This involved people of different cultural and language backgrounds, from the strictest of Jewish conservatism through to those who had little or no religious belief prior to his contact with them.

The only reason the missionary journeys were undertaken was because Paul intended to undertake a routine visit of churches previously established.[10]

The pastoral epistles came down to us because Paul wanted to immediately handle problems faced by the local congregations, to give them guidance in their personal actions and to explain some of his teachings. In one sense all of the epistles are 'pastoral' in that they are informing the church on matters pertaining to the pastoral life of the people. Even the letter to the Romans has behind it a very practical purpose: to introduce his plans to visit them and then to go on, with their help, to evangelise Spain:

I have been wanting for so many years to come to see you . . . I would like to see you on my way to Spain, and be helped by you to go there, after I have enjoyed visiting you for a while. [11]

4. Theological conflict
Paul's frequent theological conflicts and resultant pressures must have made it difficult for him to continue at the pace he had established in his ministry.

The conflicts will be discussed in more detail in Chapter 7 when we consider Paul as a philosopher. The first conflict we have already noted was with the apostle Peter and other leaders of the church concerning the reception of Gentiles into the church. Paul's viewpoint held sway and changed the history of the church. A further area concerned continual debates with people who belonged to other religions. He debated with the devotees of various Greek and Roman gods, with animists, with magicians and the believers of local superstitions. A further group were his own Jewish compatriots, particularly the ultra-conservative Pharisees, who believed that every change was a change for the worse. A final group consisted of some of the Jewish Christians who wanted to emphasise the keeping of both the old covenant with its food laws, cultural traditions, circumcision and Sabbath keeping, along with the new covenant.

There is an emotional, intellectual and physical price that comes upon a person who is constantly engaged in having to defend the faith he believes. Paul knew the burden of theological conflict.

5. Cultural conflict
The following passage indicates the way the Greeks did not like the way Paul spoke or presented himself in public: 'Paul's letters are severe and strong, but when he is with us in person, he is weak, and his words are nothing!'[12]

These terms of abuse used of Paul were also used in the ancient world of other speakers and it is quite clear that they referred to a cultural attitude the Greeks had towards people who did not speak with a correct form. One of the fundamental principles upon which the Greek status system rested, as Professor Edwin A. Judge has pointed out, 'is the belief that fine form is congruent with truth. Cultivation in the literary and artistic sense was thus a means of legitimising the status of those who could afford it and precisely because it made a conspicuous difference to a person's public appearance, it became the means by which the social inferiority of the uncultivated was imposed on them as a felt distinction.'[13] Paul quite consciously refused to accept this cultural distinction of the Greeks and identified with Jesus Christ in his weakness and rejection. Nothing that Paul did was designed to win approval of the Greek culture. Instead he stressed the foolishness of preaching.

Paul also ran into conflict because he was too independent. The Greeks objected to Paul because he would not accept their financial support and insisted instead upon working with his hands as a tentmaker to keep himself. Paul was unashamed of labour and believed that everyone should earn his own keep. This cut across the cultural traditions of the Greeks who believed that only the peasants or slaves should work and that social power was exercised not by taking profit from one's slaves, but by passing money down to them to keep up one's own dignity and position. To reject money from a person was to become an enemy as it meant that you refused to accept his superior status.

6. Distress at failing members

Any leader is distraught when key supporters fail him and let down the standards. Paul gives evidence constantly of the emotional hurt he suffered because of the failure of people whom he trusted or young leaders in whose training he had invested himself. An example of this was when Paul was planning to revisit towns where they had preached the gospel and Barnabas wanted to take John Mark with them. 'Paul did not think it right to ... take him, because he had not stayed with them to the end of their mission, but had turned back and left them in Pamphylia. There was a sharp argument, and they separated: Barnabas took Mark and sailed off for Cyprus, while Paul

chose Silas and left, commended by the believers to the care of the Lord's grace.'[14]

But it was the Christians in the local church, particularly in the churches Paul had established, such as at Corinth and in Galatia, that were to disappoint him constantly. The church at Corinth had a record for bad behaviour. Immorality was rife, and idolatry, drunkenness and stealing were known among the members. Some Christians were caught up in court cases against each other while others were involved in sexual immorality with prostitutes; other members in the same church got drunk at the Lord's Table and some undercut Paul's teaching and called him inferior and an amateur. How Paul's heart must have ached to see people who had come to know the Lord and had grown in their faith, decline in their personal standards.

Corinth

7. Pressures from a materialistic society

Paul lived in an immoral society and the church, while it was expected to influence the world, found the world influencing it. As we have seen, the church at Corinth had deep personal, sexual and social problems within it: it sounds as if every contemporary social problem was alive within that church. The pressures of a materialistic culture made it very difficult for Christians to be disciplined and pure in word and deed.

Many of the early churches found it difficult to refrain from idolatry. It was pervasive in the ancient world, as is shown in Paul's experience in Athens.[15] If a person went to the butchers to buy meat, the meat had already been offered to idols. If a person wanted to join a trade union, to offer a sacrifice to the idol was expected. If a person wanted to be part of an educational institution, or to celebrate an anniversary or even to prove his loyalty to the government, sacrifices to the idols or to Caesar were a standard practice. For many people this was purely a ritual without any significant religious connotation, but the early church refused to say that anything or anyone was Lord. Many Christians died rather than worship the idols, but there were many others, attested to by the writing of Pliny and others, who were willing to bow before an idol. Consequently the daily pressure, and the weakness of some Christians in bowing to it, was a constant drain upon Paul's emotions.

Those cultural conflicts were part of the pressures Paul felt in his leadership of the young church.

8. The pressures from the demands of disturbed and difficult people

As Peter and John found when they went to worship at the Temple, the lame were always at the gates.[16] Always the churches seem to attract people who are mentally, emotionally and psychologically lame as well as those who have deep physical and spiritual needs.

The demands of disturbed and difficult people cause many ministers not to cope with constant intellectual and emotional pressures. Paul faced such people frequently. In Lystra he found a man who was lame from birth and who desired healing. That act of compassion in healing the lame man led Barnabas and Paul into great difficulties from the people that crowded round them marvelling at their healing power. Having simply helped the lame man walk earned them eventually a riot and stoning![17]

Even friends sometimes became a burden. Epaphroditus was sent by the church at Philippi to aid Paul during his imprisonment. But unfortunately Epaphroditus caught the fever that was common in prisons and almost died. The one who was sent to help Paul ended up having to be nursed by Paul. Paul's evident relief is shown when he says: 'But God had pity on him, and not only him but on me too, and spared me an even greater sorrow.'[18] He goes on to build up Epaphroditus' image in the eyes of the congregation, speaking proudly of the work that he has done and how, in fact, his presence was fulfilling what they themselves ought to have done in helping him.

So Paul lived constantly facing disturbed and difficult people and this itself was stress-inducing.

9. The pain of constant rejection

Many people can minister valiantly under incredibly difficult circumstances if they know that somewhere their work is appreciated and that others are praying and supporting them. But Paul constantly ran into rejection even from people who should have been his keenest supporters.

We have already seen the damage that the dispute with the disciples caused when he went to Jerusalem and tried to join them. But they would not believe he was a disciple, and they were all afraid of him.[19] Later he had clashes with them over the role of the Gentiles in the church and with the leaders at Jerusalem.

There were also constantly the conflicts with Jews who totally opposed his theological understanding of the admission of Gentiles into the family of God. Those antagonistic Jews followed him everywhere, causing riots and physical attacks upon the apostles. Throughout all of his travels those Jews rejected him as a pharisee and as a teacher of their law. Paul outlines his reaction to rejection: 'When people criticise me, this is how I defend myself', and he gives a long list of the rights and duties of an apostle, even pointing out the comparison between himself and others: 'Don't I have the right to follow the example of the other apostles and the Lord's brothers and Peter, by taking a Christian wife with me on my trips? Or are Barnabas and I the only ones who have to work for our living?'[20]

Constant rejection by friend and foe alike take a heavy toll on the mental health and emotional stability of any leader, yet throughout all of his life Paul, faced with this constant rejection, showed all the signs of coping well. There is probably no greater evidence for the soundness of his body and mind, his emotions and spirit, than the fact that he was under such pressure constantly and yet was able to carry the burden with the most positive outlook, with an optimistic spirit and able consistently to sing the goodness of God towards him.

What enabled Paul to cope under such pressure?

A careful study once more of the written record indicates not only the pressures under which Paul operated but the resources which he used to enable him to cope with those pressures.

1. He accepted God's call for him

Paul was in ministry because he couldn't possibly be anywhere else. God had called him to that work and the assurance of his call held him fast. Inevitably people who burn out under pressure are those who lack assurance of their own calling. But Paul had no hesitation: the God who called him into this work would strengthen him and enable him to fulfil the task before him.

There were others who questioned that calling but Paul repeatedly reiterated it in his addresses, his disputes and debates, and in the letters he sent. 'I am speaking now to you Gentiles: as long as I am an apostle to the Gentiles, I will take pride in my work.'[21] The high sense of calling constantly strengthened him giving him patience and endurance under the attacks of opponents and small-minded people.

Stairs at the Roman Colosseum

2. He believed in the significance of his work

Inevitably ministers and workers for God who suffer from emotional and spiritual fatigue question the worthwhileness of their effort.

But there was no questioning with Paul. He had a strong conviction of the significance of what he was doing: 'I reckon my own life to be worth nothing to me; I only want to complete my mission and finish the work that the Lord Jesus gave me to do, which is to declare the Good News about the grace of God.'[22] The overwhelming conviction that what he was doing was of eternal significance held him fast.

Paul was proud of his call to be a minister in the service of Christ and that gave him confidence not only to look his enemies in the eye, but to walk boldly through places of danger. 'I have been bold because of the privilege God has given me of being a servant of Christ Jesus to work for the Gentiles. I serve like a priest in preaching the Good News from God, in order that the Gentiles may be an offering acceptable to God, dedicated to him by the Holy Spirit. In union with Christ Jesus, then, I can be proud of my service for God.'[23]

Consequently his belief in the significance of his work enabled him to accept suffering and hardship as the price for the privilege of preaching the gospel. 'I am most happy, then, to be proud of my weaknesses, in order to feel the protection of Christ's power over me. I am content with weaknesses, insults, hardships, persecutions, and difficulties, for Christ's sake. For when I am

weak, then I am strong.'[24]

Nothing could stop him. And even that one last great fear that holds many men back, death itself, was nothing but a doorway up to which Paul would march boldly still preaching. He was prepared to 'pour out my life's blood like an offering on the sacrifice that your faith offers to God. If that is so, I am glad and I share my joy with you all.'[25]

Nothing can stop a person who believes in the eternal significance of his work.

3. He committed his life to the work of the gospel

Commitment for Paul was a lifetime commitment and not an emotional response. It was an act of will which carried him through the most difficult of hardships.

When a person commits his life in marriage, for better or for worse, for richer or for poorer, in sickness and in health, the commitment is designed to show loyalty and fidelity regardless of the circumstances. It was that same kind of commitment that Paul made to the gospel. 'We are often troubled, but not crushed; sometimes in doubt, but never in despair; and there are many enemies, but we are never without a friend; and though badly hurt at times, we are not destroyed . . . for this reason we never become discouraged. Even though our physical being is gradually decaying, yet our spiritual being is renewed day by day.'[26]

One aspect of helping people under pressure to cope today is to encourage them to renew their vows of commitment when as an act of will they determine to continue their calling.

4. He disciplined his desires

One reason many people do not last in any kind of demanding work is that there is a conflict between the work they are doing and other areas of their life. Like all people who work with their eyes fixed upon a goal, Paul did not allow himself to be diverted into any area of ill-discipline of thought, emotion or relationship.

He wrote to the Thessalonians: 'We worked day and night so that we would not be any trouble to you as we preached to you the Good News from God . . . we were not lazy when we were with you. We did not accept anyone's support without paying for it.'[27]

What becomes obvious when his writings are looked at with fresh eyes is that he had a good balance between his sense of the significance of his calling and his modesty as to his own personal attainments. He was able to boast but he boasted within limits. This aspect of discipline gives us an indication of the true meaning of humility; a humble man knows his own significance and worth yet does not boast of his own attainments.

Note how Paul expressed this:

When I came to you, my brothers, to preach God's secret truth, I did not use big words, and great learning. For while I was with you, I made up my mind to forget everything except Jesus Christ and especially his death on the cross. So when I came to you, I was weak and trembled all over with fear, and my teaching and message were not delivered with skilful words of human wisdom, but with convincing proof of the power of God's Spirit. Your faith, then, does not rest on human wisdom but upon God's power.[28]

As for us, our boasting will not go beyond certain limits; it will stay within the limits of the work which God has set for us, and this includes our work among you . . . we hope that your faith may grow and that we may be able to do a much greater work among you, always within the limits God has set.[29]

In guiding new Christians Paul sometimes referred to his own sense of personal discipline as a means of encouraging others to become more efficient in their Christian life and more committed in their service.

I am like a boxer who does not waste his punches. I harden my body with blows and bring it under complete control to keep myself from being disqualified after having called others to the contest.[30]

Paul was able to cope with heavy burdens of responsibility because of the way he disciplined himself, his appetites and his desires.

5. He witnessed enthusiastically

Paul had enormous enthusiasm for talking to other people about Jesus Christ.

From the day when they met on the Damascus road, Paul was obsessed with the desire to tell other people about Jesus who had turned his life right round. He witnessed to friends and acquaintances, to enemies and aggressors, to soldiers and sailors, to guards on duty, and to kings sitting in judgment; in the early hours of the morning and at midnight, in the midst of an earthquake and a storm at sea: there was no time or place or person where it was not appropriate for him to witness to Jesus Christ.

Church at Acro-Corinth

6. He fashioned a bond of caring with his people

One of the incredible resources a person engaged in God's work has that enables him to cope with all kinds of pressures is the strength that comes from what we call *Christian fellowship*. Paul built a relationship between himself and those who became believers that became richer over the years. As ministers and pastors testify, those that build a bond of caring with their people find that, far from becoming a burden, that bond of caring is a support and encouragement to them in all that they do.

Paul's longest ministry covered the three years he spent at Ephesus. He really loved those people and when he was passing near Ephesus before returning to Jerusalem where he would be arrested and eventually taken to Rome for trial, 'Paul sent a message to Ephesus, asking the elders of the church to meet him. At that meeting they reflected upon the times they had shared together and when Paul finished, he knelt down with them and prayed.[31]

The bond of caring for people was demonstrated in many ways such as his emphasis on the strong needing to help the weak in the faith, and in his determination that the widows and orphans be cared for. Those who feel burnt out because of the pressures of their work would do well to remember all of those for whom they care and those who reciprocate that care. The bonds of fellowship in a Christian church are very strong and provide a marvellous resource for those people who feel alone and threatened.

7. He gained strength from the support of his friends

Like many people throughout history who have been known for their strong stands and very definite views, Paul not only raised enemies, but he created friends who were willing to stick beside him through the most difficult of circumstances. Those friends greatly helped and encouraged him throughout his ministry. Many in the church today do not recognise either the number or the names of those people whom Paul acknowledges were special friends. The names of Sopater, Aristarchus, Secundus, Gaius, Tychicus, Trophimus, are nowhere as well known as Timothy, Silas, Barnabas and John Mark. But each of these spent time serving Paul. In Romans chapter 16, Paul sends personal greetings to some twenty-one people in a city he had not personally visited. Yet he knew those people and many of them he refers to as his fellow workers or fellow prisoners. When he wrote his letter to the church at Colossae, he commended a number of people in the church for what they had done to support him and described them as fellow workers and fellow servants. These people included Tychicus, Onesimus, Aristarchus, Mark, Joshua, Epaphras, Luke and Demas among others. Whether they were with him in prison or there in the churches praying for him, Paul gained strength from the support of his friends.

It is hard for people to be overwhelmed by the pressures of work when they are surrounded by supportive friends.

8. He held fast to the scriptures

This is one of the great secrets found over the years by those who have withstood the greatest of pressures. Those who have to live and work under immense emotional, psychological and spiritual pressure find the refreshment that comes constantly through the scriptures. It was the constant study of the scriptures that held Martin Luther fast and enabled him to stand. On every mission field in the world, faithful men and women under attack and acute pressure have found that their surest resource in time of stress has been the spiritual nourishment that comes from the scriptures.

Paul was a keen student of the scriptures and he meditated on the words and teachings of Jesus. A list of all the quotations found in the epistles and in the speeches of Paul is indeed a very long and intricate one, showing his knowledge of the law, the psalms, and the prophets in particular. I have counted thirty-five major quotations from the Old Testament in his speeches and letters.

It was the scriptures that gave him insights into every aspect of the life, teachings and personal significance of Jesus. By keeping close to the scriptures Paul found a resource that enabled him to cope with the pressures of ministry.

9. He lived boldly

There was nothing half-hearted about Paul's approach to his work. He was fully committed, proud of his calling and willing to go ahead with great boldness. That boldness generated within him strength and enthusiasm that enabled him to cope with the constant problems that beset him. 'So we are always full of courage. We know that as long as we are at home in the body we are away from the Lord's home . . . we are full of courage and would much prefer to leave our home in the body and be at home with the Lord.'[32]

Paul was prepared to be bold before kings and governors, before crowds and individuals. When he was defending himself before the Sanhedrin the high priest, Ananias, ordered someone to strike Paul on the mouth because of the boldness with which he was speaking. But Paul quickly put the high priest in his place. Nothing could silence him because he was confident that God would help him in every time of trouble.

Paul testified constantly that God always helps us in our trials and that we need to boldly witness to our faith knowing that God will never allow us to be left utterly alone. 'He will not allow you to be tested beyond your power to remain firm; at the time you are put to the test he will give you the strength to endure it, and so provide you with a way out.'[33]

From the presence of God Paul gained strength, confidence and boldness to live in spite of difficulty. It was that divine assurance that enabled him to cope.

10. He did not carry false guilt

One reason that many people collapse under the strain is that they frequently have feelings of guilt, of personal failure and a consciousness of moral wrong.

Paul had the overwhelming conviction that Christ had died for his sins and had forgiven him everything. Consequently he never carried a burden of guilt about either what he had done in the past or during the time when he persecuted the church of God.

Paul was quite willing to share the gospel with people but he didn't feel a false guilt if they rejected what he had to say. He knew he had fulfilled his part and therefore there was no reason that he should feel the burden of unfulfilled hopes. On one occasion, Paul protested at the people's opposition 'by shaking the dust from his clothes and saying to them: "If you are lost, you yourselves must take the blame for it! I am not responsible." '34

It takes very emotionally secure and spiritually mature people to be able to free themselves from the burden of such false guilt and also have such a compassion for people and commitment to the task of witnessing.

Being free from any feeling of false guilt enabled Paul to carry even heavier burdens. The totally free person, who is confident of his own personal forgiveness by the Lord, can be of tremendous use in witnessing of the faith to others.

As a pastor Paul knew the cost of caring. In our day and age many are burning out because of the pressures of pastoring. But Paul's personal example indicates that the minister of God can cope with enormous pressures without collapsing under them if he also matches to those pressures the resources that God provides.

For personal reading

Theme: The pastoral ministry

MONDAY
In humility, give God the glory
1 Corinthians 3:3-9 and Romans 12:3-4

TUESDAY
Confidence in God's faithfulness
1 Corinthians 10:6-13

WEDNESDAY
The need for discipline
1 Corinthians 9:24-27 and Philippians 3:12-16

THURSDAY
Sorrowing for sinners
Galatians 4:11-20

FRIDAY
Be worthy of the gospel
1 Thessalonians 5:12-25

SATURDAY
Dangers in the ministry
2 Corinthians 11:21-33

SUNDAY
Grateful for co-workers
Philippians 1:1-11

For group study

Topic: The cost of caring

1 In what ways can we help faithful men of God overcome 'burn-out' and vocational despair?

2 Identify pressures that ministers of the church face today. Do you know any of God's servants today who are being pressured?

3 Paul identified with the personal struggles of his flock. Can we care for someone without being involved?

4 What do you do with people who are quarrelsome and disruptive in behaviour? Can you face rejection and ridicule?

5 What can we learn from Paul's sense of calling and commitment to be the pastor of a flock?

6 What character traits would be necessary to be an effective carer of people?

5

Paul the Pioneer

I was a newly ordained minister when I invited Henry Chan, an international student, to my home for a meal. He listened very politely to my talking about Jesus and then said: 'My father does not believe your religion and he has taught me to believe the religions of my ancestors. If what you say about Jesus is true, why didn't your father or grandfather come and tell my father and my grandfather?' I explained to him that my father was not a Christian and that the message had needed to be taken to him as well.

Henry then nailed me to the wall: 'But if your Jesus told you to take this message to all the peoples in the world why have you been so disobedient all these centuries, and why are you still among your own people when my people have not yet heard about him?'

Henry had touched the Achilles heel of many ministers and most churches. During the latter part of the twentieth century the church has been experiencing a harvest time. The church has been growing at a rate of 63,000 new converts per day, with currently 285,421 full-time Christian workers in Asia, 431,321 in Africa, 253,702 in Latin America and 1,059,742 in Europe. The number of full-time workers producing the Christian harvest around the world is most disproportionately spread. In North America there is one Christian worker for every 1,321 people, whereas in Africa the ratio is one worker for 249,278 people.[1] Many of the 16,750 separate cultural groupings in the world are amongst the 4 billion peoples in Asia, Africa and Latin America and many of these groupings have not heard the gospel. Cross-cultural missionary endeavour on a large scale is needed to spread the gospel among the many unreached peoples of the earth.

The nineteenth century was the great era of Christian missions. Throughout that century hundreds of thousands of men and women were motivated to serve in foreign lands or to support overseas missionaries. The nineteenth century was moved when David Livingstone, missionary, explorer and philanthropist, died in the village of a friendly African chief in 1873. The Africans called a conference of all the village men and decided 'we must take the master back to the coast and across the sea to his own people', so they set out on a thousand-mile journey by foot carrying his body to the coast from whence it was shipped to England, reaching Westminster Abbey just one year later. This action made a great impression.

The example of missionaries like Livingstone led to a vast number of interdenominational Christian missionary movements. One, the Student Volunteer Movement, saw in the last decade of the nineteenth century 20,000 volunteers go overseas with the message of the gospel. Their one cry was 'the evangelisation of the world in our generation.'

They took the command of Jesus, known as the great commission — 'Go, then, to all peoples everywhere and make them my disciples' — and went out to reach every country on earth with the gospel. Jesus made it quite clear he expected his people to proclaim the gospel, and to make disciples of all nations. That same conviction was carried through in the lives and letters of Paul and Peter and the other New Testament Christians.

The primary task of the missionary effort was to bring individuals to salvation in Christ, so that they might believe and be baptised as a sign of forgiveness of sins, the Lordship of Christ and incorporation into the church. The missionaries also served every kind of human need, creating eighty-five per cent of all schools in Africa, more than 600 hospitals in India, and bringing the benefits of education, medicine and social enlightenment to every country on earth.

That commission of Jesus has never been revoked.

Today we speak of *frontier missions*: taking the good news to people in other cultures who have not yet responded to the Christian gospel. We also speak of *domestic missions*: sharing the message among those people of our own culture who have not yet responded. There are no longer just sending churches and receiving churches. Every church needs to be a church in mission, both on the domestic and the frontier planes.

In spite of the large numbers not yet reached, the great commission is not an unfinishable task. It can be accomplished if we continue the missionary task of the church as Paul started it.

The book of Acts is the first handbook on domestic and frontier missions. It outlines the practices and principles for each generation of cross-cultural missions. The example of Paul in establishing the missionary outreach of the church is as relevant today as to the first century.

The mission of the church
Christ's last command, the great commission of Jesus, 'To all peoples everywhere', became Paul's first concern. From the time of his conversion he believed that he had been chosen to take the gospel to all people.[2] To the Roman Christians he said that 'the truth has been brought out into the open through the writings of the prophets; and by the command of the eternal God it is made known to all nations, so that all may believe and obey.'[3] In writing this Paul used the same unique Greek phrase that Jesus used in giving the great commission to his disciples.

The failure of Israel as a nation to attract people to God as creator and ruler and her rejection of the messengers of God led ultimately to God sending his only Son. The parable of the vineyard and the introduction to the book of Hebrews are two New Testament points that link the method of the coming of Jesus with that of the fulfilment of Israel's mission to the world. The church, as the new Israel, was to bear the message of God brought by his Son. Jesus commissioned his people to take that message to the uttermost parts of the earth.

Their task was no less than the evangelisation of the world. It is important to realise that there is no separate theology of mission.

It is not an appendix to biblical theology, but part of its very heart. The church was given the task to take the gospel and make it known to all people. However, the limitations of culture, of education and of vision meant none of the eleven original disciples, nor even James, Jesus' brother, had the dynamism and preparation to fulfil that mission beyond their own culture.

God required a new man with specific training, skills and motivation to launch the Christian missionary thrust. That man was Paul.

Philippi

Arch of Crusader Castle
on Acro-Corinth: Greece

The leadership of the Holy Spirit
The disciples had been
eyewitnesses of the great decisive
redemptive act of God through
Jesus. They believed that what
was happening was in complete
harmony with the teaching of
God's mission as outlined in the
Old Testament. They believed
that this was to benefit all of
mankind dependent only upon a
receptive faith-obedience to the
gospel. This teaching is apparent

in the following passage: 'The
God of our ancestors raised Jesus
from death, after you had killed
him by nailing him to a cross.
God raised him to his right side
as Leader and Saviour, to give the
people of Israel the opportunity to
repent and have their sins
forgiven. We are witnesses to
these things — we and the Holy
Spirit, who is God's gift to those
who obey him.'[4]
  They now had to take this
message to everybody who would
hear. The commission of Christ

was given to them like a pair of sandals. They should now set out upon the road and keep going until all people heard the story of what they had witnessed.

The dynamic that motivated the apostles was the equipping of the Holy Spirit. On the day of Pentecost, in a new way, the Spirit of God equipped and empowered the disciples to fulfil their mission to the world. Through the presence of the Holy Spirit the mission of God had a new dynamism. The 'Come' of the Old Testament was replaced by the 'Go' of the New Testament.

The Holy Spirit was the power that made the men go in mission. On the day of Pentecost Peter preached to many listeners including visitors from Rome and from all the countries around. Many of those who believed and who were baptised must have taken the message of the resurrected Christ back to their homes. Phillip went to Samaria and stopped in Caesarea, evangelising the community round about him on the coast. Peter had contact with Simon the Tanner at Joppa, mingling with a believer who handled dead animals which was contrary to the law, surely an amazing enough event for a man who kept the law. Peter met with Cornelius, a Roman army captain who also had the spirit of God and in the remarkable meeting with this Roman Peter came to the following conclusion: 'I now realise that it is true that God treats everyone on the same basis. Whoever fears him and does what is right is acceptable to him, no matter what race he belongs to.'[5]

Unknown believers who were scattered by the persecution which took place when Stephen was killed, settled in Phoenicia, Cyprus and Antioch. It was there that the faith expanded and the believers were first called Christians.

The Jewish believers in Jerusalem were quite concerned about what was happening with these Greek-speaking Jews living in Gentile territory. So they sent Barnabas to Antioch. When Barnabas saw that the believers were within the faith and motivated by the Holy Spirit, he went on to Tarsus and after much searching found Saul and brought him back to Antioch where the two of them taught the believers for a whole year. Here we have, for the first time, a church growing outside of Israel.

All of this growth took place under the leadership of the Holy Spirit.

Dedicated to the Gentiles

Paul maintained right from the moment of his conversion that he was called to take the message to the Gentiles, a fact he made clear on the occasions when he recounted his conversion. He told Luke who recorded it in the Acts of the Apostles that, when he was stopped by the resurrected Christ on the Damascus road, he was told to go into the city where it would be told to him what he must do. At the same time Ananias said that the Lord had said to him, 'Go, because I have chosen [Paul] to serve me, to make my name known to the Gentiles and kings and to the people of Israel.'[6]

Paul's primary concern was that of an evangelist, to win as many people to Christ as possible. In order to be an effective missionary evangelist, he adapted to the different peoples he worked amongst.

I make myself everybody's slave in order to win as many people as possible. While working with the Jews, I live like a Jew in order to win them. In the same way, when working with Gentiles, I live like a Gentile, outside the Jewish law, in order to win Gentiles. This does not mean that I don't obey God's law; I am really under Christ's law. Among the weak in faith I become weak like one of them, in order to win them. So I become all things to all men, that I may save some of them by whatever means are possible.[7]

According to Paul's memory, in this earliest time of his ministry several aspects were clear in his mind:

1. God had chosen him to proclaim his message to all people.
2. He had a special responsibility to travel far distances to proclaim God's gospel to the Gentiles.
3. He would suffer at the hands of the Gentiles but that God would deliver him from their hands.
4. His ministry would take him to the uttermost parts of the world.

This concern to care for those who are outside the Jewish family found in Paul a man equipped and able. God had chosen well when he took a man born within the Jewish tradition, trained in Greek culture who possessed Roman citizenship, and with some of the best intellectual and philosophical training that the ancient world had to offer. That man was to open up the countries of the Mediterranean to the gospel.

After Barnabas found him ministering in Tarsus, Paul returned for a brief one-year ministry in Antioch. There together they served, helping the first Gentile church in the world develop in faith and strength. That church possessed five leaders, three prophets and two teachers, and the interesting thing was that they came from five countries. It was while these leaders were praying and fasting that the Holy Spirit declared to them: 'Set apart for me Barnabas and Saul, to do the work to which I have called them'.[8] After fasting, praying and having hands laid on them in a commissioning to ministry, these two men were sent by the Holy Spirit on the first journey throughout the Mediterranean area, commencing at Cyprus which Barnabas knew so well.

Throughout the rest of his life Paul would contend that he had been called from the time of his conversion to preach the gospel to the Gentiles and commissioned by the leaders of the church at Antioch by the laying on of hands and prayer to that missionary service. For instance, when he wrote to the Christians in Rome he said, 'I will be bold and speak only about what Christ has done through me to lead the Gentiles to obey God.'[9]

Later when Paul and Barnabas came to Jerusalem for the famous conference with the leaders of the church, there was some discussion about which fields each of the disciples should enter. They recognised that Paul's gospel was true to their experience of Jesus but that he had a special commission to preach to the Gentiles beyond that of their own general call to take the gospel into the known world. To the farmers and fishermen of Galilee it must have been of some relief to find one who was sophisticated in the ways of the world who was eager to take up this part of the Lord's great commission. As Paul said, 'We agreed that Barnabas and I would work among the Gentiles, and they would work among the Jews. All they asked was that we should remember the needy in their group, which is the very thing I have been eager to do.'[10]

While Peter was later to visit some of the Jewish centres in Greece and Rome, he would also visit the Gentile Christians in that area. In the same way while Paul was primarily called to proclaim the truth to the Gentiles, he would also go to the Jewish communities he found in the cities he visited. Hence the demarcation into ministries among Jews and Gentiles was not exclusive but indicated the areas of primary emphasis.

Paul regarded the rest of the world as his area of ministry while leaving the other disciples to evangelise the homeland.

Pioneering in Philippi

One night, while in Troas, Paul had a vision in which he saw a man from Macedonia begging him to 'come over to Macedonia and help us'[11] Luke now travelled with them. Although Paul was strongly motivated by the vision in the night, Luke, a young man from Macedonia, probably helped persuade them to take the gospel to his people in Europe.

Paul and his companions, Timothy, Silas and Luke, had favourable winds and crossed over to Neapolis in one day. A few years later, when Paul sailed in the reverse direction, it took him five days to cover the same distance. They then walked the dozen or so kilometres down the Via Egnatia to the township of Philippi, named after Philip of Macedon, the father of Alexander the Great. This major provincial centre was not only steeped in Greek history but was a significant Roman colony.

It is interesting to see how Paul developed a strategy in a new community.

1. He approached the people openly. He quickly met with the citizens in the community, going first of all to the Jewish people who were willing to accept him as a learned pharisee able to proclaim the truth.

2. He preached the whole gospel speaking of Jewish history to those who were Jews and moving on to Christ as the fulfilment of the prophecies. The four of them, Paul, Timothy, Silas and Luke, proclaimed the truth in the open air, for apparently the community lacked the ten Jewish males necessary in order to be allowed to build their own synagogue.

Boat harbour at Philippi

3. He was God's agent in bringing about conversions. Paul met with a small group of Jews worshipping by the riverside under the leadership of Lydia, a widow from Thyatira in Central Turkey. The ruins of the Roman bridge over the River Ganga dating from the first century have recently been excavated. It was at this spot about a mile down the Via Egnatia where the Jews would worship. She was a wealthy woman who had a good business dealing in the exclusive purple cloth that came from that district which was worn by leading citizens. It was probably while she was in Thyatira, where there was a large synagogue, that she became a God-fearer, worshipping with the Jewish community. Her business acumen and wealth were probably the reason why four times Paul received gifts during his imprisonments from what was otherwise a very poor church. He proclaimed the gospel in such a way that she believed and was immediately baptised.[12] Lydia invited the four men to her home and there she grew in her faith and into the position of leadership within the church.

A second conversion in Philippi happened that night in the most unusual way. At midnight while singing hymns of praise the prison was shaken by an earthquake and the chains fell off, not only of Paul and Silas, but also of the other prisoners. The Roman gaoler in Roman fashion attempted to kill himself, as he had failed in his duty to keep his prisoners and had instead been asleep. Paul prevented his suicide, took the opportunity to proclaim the faith, and eventually, while they were cleaned up in the gaoler's own house, baptised him and his family.

It is possible that Euodia, Syntyche and Clement also became Christians at this time. Paul enabled the conversions of a number of people, and by the time he and Silas left there was a good number of believers gathering regularly in Lydia's house.

4. He worked among all social classes. Among the first converts in Philippi were representatives of different races, different classes and people representing different economic conditions and educational backgrounds. They needed pastoring to build a church that already was multi-cultural. Consequently Luke stayed behind in the city that he knew so well and helped build the church. Perhaps he is the 'true yoke fellow' to whom Paul addresses a word of commendation when he wrote a letter to that church some years later.[13]

5. He faced opposition. There were the slave owners who were fearful at their loss of revenue. There were the unjust magistrates (praetors) who had Paul beaten by the lictors (who carried their rods of office with an axe bundled together as seen frequently in Roman illustrations).

6. He planned for future church growth. Having established a church in an important provincial centre, Paul moved on to establish further churches at Thessalonica and Berea and on to Athens. Paul saw his ministry as one of planting churches. He then left behind suitable leaders: either young ministers like Timothy or

Luke, or else appointed elders to oversee the life of the church. Paul's concern was to evangelise the larger cities (urbes) and then send his travelling ministers into the areas beyond (sub-urbes). This strategy of penetration enabled the whole province to be reached with the gospel while he moved on, establishing new churches in each important centre.

7. He moved on with optimism. Having left Philippi with Luke in charge, Paul moved on to new challenges and hardships. Training young men in leadership he delegated responsibilities while he continued with the spirit of the pioneer.

He continued through Greece until he came to Athens. Along the way more adventures, more establishment of churches and more personal opposition. Paul the pioneer was blazing the trail into the whole of Europe. Christianity would now never again be locked within the land of Israel or within the tradition of the Jews. He had broken out of the culture of the people that had given birth to Jesus, and had thrust his faith into the centre of the continent which would be the centre of civilisation for the next two thousand years.

Paul the pioneer was following the example of his Lord Jesus Christ, who was himself the pioneer of our faith.[14]

Cross-cultural ministries today

The church is God's agent for mission. It is to perform for the world the service of being a witness to the kingdom of God which has come and which is coming in Jesus Christ. It is impossible to separate the church from its mission. The church is only the church when it is the church in mission. The church is God's agent on earth through which God expresses himself to the world, and God has no other redeeming agency. When people are called to come to Christ, they are called to come to his body, the community of believers, to take his message to all others.

The colonial missionary era is over, but the era of world mission has just begun. Both in domestic mission and frontier mission the church has a global responsibility as its primary task. That witness is evangelical and social, private and public, individual and corporate.

The rapid growth of population in countries which have not yet had the gospel clearly presented requires that the twentieth century church move into high gear if it is to fulfil the great commission. Here is the new challenge: a church for every people by the bi-millennium! By the year 2,000 it should be our responsibility to see that every separate cultural group on earth has the opportunity to hear the good news personally.

There have been three surges in the church's missionary movement. The first, in the eighteenth century, was the denominational missionary societies; the second surge, in the mid-nineteenth century, was the interdenominational societies; a third surge began in the church's missionary task in the nineteen-fifties.The middle of the twentieth century had begun to reveal the hidden peoples of the earth — those groups which are divided from others even within their own country by custom, race, economic and geographic circumstances. These include the large number of Japanese living in the USA, along with several million Koreans and Samoans. Ethnic groups are to be found in most countries. The Moroccans constitute a large people group in France, the Turks are in Germany, the Jamaicans are in London, the Vietnamese are in Sydney and so on. The church now has charted the existence and computerised the strategy to reach every one of the 16,750 hidden groups around the world.

The apostle Paul has given us the example of cross-cultural missionaries. Christians today should ask the following questions to see if they might be called by God to proclaim his message as did the early apostles:

☐ Do I love the Lord sufficiently to leave my family, friends and the security of my home to take the message to someone else?

☐ Can I relate to other people of different cultures, races, languages and customs enough to learn their language, eat their food and understand their thought forms?

☐ Can I communicate adequately my faith with people of my own culture and in my own language, for could I really expect to communicate well with others if I cannot communicate to my own first?

☐ Am I healthy and able to live a fairly rugged, independent life in spite of hepatitis, typhoid, dysentery, malaria and colitis, which can so easily affect people in the Two-thirds World?

☐ Am I willing to serve, not counting the cost, being willing to stand periods of isolation and to bear heavy burdens of responsibility without having someone close at hand, or at the end of a telephone, to make decisions for me?

☐ Do I have some skills, not just in the traditional areas of medicine and education, but in any other field, that might be of help in frontier missions?

☐ Am I able to survive on my own without becoming depressed or lonely and therefore seeking solace in romance or alcohol, or any of the hundred other ways that could deflect me from my task of proclaiming the gospel of Jesus Christ?

The church today is facing the challenge of having *a church available for every people by the bi-millennium!*

Paul's pioneering work is still unfinished, but it is finishable — if enough people go!

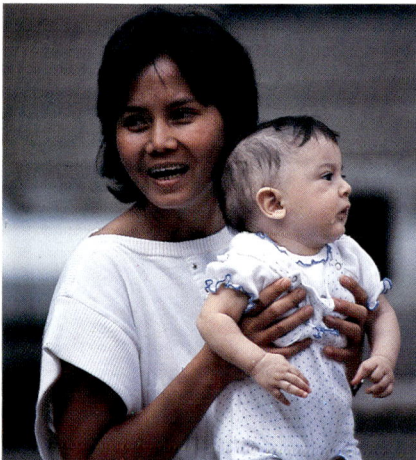

For personal reading

Theme: Spread of the gospel

MONDAY — The great commission
Matthew 28:16-20 and Acts 1:6-8

TUESDAY — Obedient to the Holy Spirit
Acts 13:1-12

WEDNESDAY — Courage to preach
Acts 18:5-11

THURSDAY — Paul's calling
Acts 22:17-21 and Galatians 2:6-10

FRIDAY — Gospel for all nations
Romans 16:25-27 and Romans 10:11-21

SATURDAY — Christianity expands
Acts 11:19-30

SUNDAY — Zeal in the Lord
1 Corinthians 9:19-22 and 2 Corinthians 1:15-22

For group study

Topic: Christian message and church growth

1 Jesus gave a missionary command. What is expected of an ordinary Christian disciple?

2 What must be the core of the missionary message? What is mission in today's context?

3 What is the authority of the evangelist?

4 Paul reached Europe through Asia Minor (Turkey). Can you highlight some of the important events which took place during this part of his missionary outreach?

5 How would you describe Paul's strategy for growth? Can they be applied today in our own situation?

6 What is meant by cross-cultural ministry? Does God call you to be his witness where you are?

6

Paul the Protagonist

A recent survey of 3,000 university students examined their fears. The three greatest fears they faced were having to stand to give a speech in public, the fear of failure and the fear of dying. All other fears were rated quite lowly.

The fear of having to stand up and speak about your faith is a fear shared by many Christians. At times when our faith is under attack and there is opposition to what we believe, many Christians feel they are unable to cope. They remain silent in the face of opposition, and subsequently are overwhelmed by guilt.

The apostle Paul was willing at any time to give a defence of his beliefs. He was also willing to go on the offensive and talk about his faith. When we combine this with the fact that we know he was regarded as a poor speaker in public and reticent to speak before people, we have an interesting paradox.

The aspect of personality that pulled Paul over his natural objections to witnessing to other people and facing opponents was his spirit as a protagonist. The Oxford Dictionary defines a protagonist as 'one who champions a cause'. For Paul, the cause was Jesus Christ and he became the first and greatest champion.

The Greek word that describes both Paul's defence of his faith and the way he was willing to go on the offensive to talk about his faith is *apologia*. In English this word is used of an 'apologist' of the faith — someone who practises an *apologia* — defending what he believes and going on the attack affirming what he knows to be true. Paul used this word several times such as when he said, 'brothers and fathers, listen to me as I make my defence (*apologia*) before you.'[1]

If we learn how Paul proclaimed his faith and defended himself from attack we, in our turn, will learn how to cope with opposition.

Paul's defence of his faith

Paul was willing to defend his faith, but he was not a pugnacious person, always wanting to get into a fight or an argument or a dispute. He was a reluctant controversialist.

Theologians have frequently looked at the way Paul defended his faith using his insights as a trained pharisee, a philosopher and a teacher, and have sought to build a case that distinguishes between the simple teaching and preaching of Jesus and that theology which was expounded by Paul. This shows a misunderstanding of Paul's thinking. When we examine his teachings closely, we realise that Paul was very conscious of the person, work and worth of Jesus Christ and understood his teachings in detail.

(a) Paul struggled with his old Jewish associates

These were the Jewish leaders who believed that Paul was committing heresy, who had opposed Stephen, and who were strongly resisting the changes of teaching and orthodoxy about which Jesus so compellingly spoke.

Paul faced two basic problems: his fellow Jews refused to accept Jesus Christ as the Messiah, and they rejected the Christians as the people of God.

The orthodox Jews saw Jesus as a political failure, a collaborator with undesirables, crucified as a criminal, belonging to an unorthodox priesthood, and concerned with people outside of the faith and the race! So they rejected him as Messiah.

They also rejected the faith because they could not conceive that an unusual group of slaves, fishermen, farmers and an occasional intellectual could be the basis of God's new people, the family of the new Israel, and the first citizens of the kingdom of God.

Paul's relationships with the Jewish race will be discussed in more detail in the chapter on Paul as a patriot. However, the rejection by the Jews of his day of himself and the other apostles was just as real as their rejection of Jesus which ended in his crucifixion.

(b) Paul also struggled with the other Jewish Christians

Among the earliest Christians, there were some who clung tenaciously to their Jewish traditions, customs and culture and wanted any who came within the church likewise to observe, as well as their new faith in Christ, the Jewish culture and customs. This struggle was the first major struggle that the church encountered. It was seen in Peter's conflict and growth in his own mind about how Gentiles should be accepted into the church. His encounter with Cornelius became the turning point when he saw that God's Spirit dwelt in the heart of the Gentile as much as in the Jew. Paul had seen this from the time of his conversion on the Damascus road and had dedicated his life to taking the gospel message to the Gentiles. For a long time, however, there was a reluctance by other Christians back in Jerusalem, where conservatism was at its height, to accept Paul's way of treating the Gentiles.

The leading exponent of this emphasis upon Jewish culture and custom for the early Christians was James, the brother of Jesus, who gradually assumed leadership within the church in Jerusalem.

There was much about the Jewish faith that was important for Christians to understand. The Jews had a very comprehensive code of moral behaviour and, in a very licentious world, the best of the Jews lived a beautifully moral life. The early Christians needed to separate themselves from the immorality of the rest of the pagan world because their lifestyle was contrary to the Law of God, both Jewish and Christian. This moral quality in their lives attracted many in the Roman and Greek world who became sick of the self-indulgent lifestyle and found the simplicity and happiness of the family life of Christians and Jews something to be envied.

James strongly emphasised the quality of Christian life. 'What God the Father considers to be pure and genuine religion is this: to take care of orphans and widows in their suffering and to keep oneself from being corrupted by the world.'[2] The Epistle of James is a collection of examples of how a person must behave and the teachings of James emphasised practical Christianity and a quality of conduct that avoided prejudice, gossip, pride, quarrelling, boasting and the like.

Paul went to the heart of the matter when he stressed that our faith was not simply a matter of decent living but first and foremost of personal acceptance of what Christ has completed on our behalf on the cross. The Christians in the early church had a conflict with Paul over his emphasis upon people being made just by the grace of God through their faith, when the teaching of James seemed so practical and pure for their promiscuous world. The emphasis was different, but both were important aspects of the Christian faith.

(c) *Paul was also troubled by opposing leaders who struggled for their position of power within the church*

His letters frequently bristle with comments about people who are seeking leadership within the church, but who are doing so from wrong motives. This is particularly true of his letters to the churches at Philippi, Corinth and in Galatia.[3]

So Paul constantly had to defend his faith, with much of his time taken up championing the cause. He needed to defend his understanding of the gospel from attacks by his old Jewish associates who refused to accept either Jesus as the Messiah or his followers as the new people of Israel. He had troubles with the leaders of the church who did not understand fully enough and quickly enough the significance of the Gentiles who came into the fullness of the Holy Spirit and therefore into the life of the church. He further had trouble with those false leaders within the church who constantly visited the churches where he had established the faith and sought to convert the new believers back into the old habits and traditions of the Jewish faith.

There is little recorded active opposition to Paul from non-Jewish and non-church sources. Certainly the Roman government, Greek educators and philosophers, local authorities, shopkeepers, showmen and magicians showed some sporadic objections to his teaching when it threatened their profits and power. There was lack of active, consistent opposition, however, partly because the Roman authorities, although not viewing Christianity as 'true religion' — a term they used for their own — treated it as a tolerated superstition at this time. During the last decade of Paul's life, however, the attitude was changing. Because Christians were believed to be guilty of a whole range of criminal and anti-social behaviour, restrictions were placed on them and they were required to sacrifice to and acknowledge the Roman state gods. They refused to do this and many, Paul amongst them, were martyred. The scriptures do not deal with this period. So we shall here concern ourselves with Paul's opponents within Judaism and the church.

Colosseum: Rome

The causes of the clashes

Although we have dealt with these issues in some detail, it would be well to look again at the causes of the clashes.

These issues came to a head on the occasions when Paul visited Jerusalem to confer with those he called the pillars of the church. On one occasion — probably the time he brought some famine relief when he and Barnabas came down from Antioch with money for the poor Christians of Jerusalem — he apparently had conflict with Peter and the other disciples over the role of Gentiles within the church and of the necessity for circumcision. Fourteen years later there was a further visit to the church leaders in Jerusalem. We assume that this was the council of the church held in Jerusalem when circumcision was the major topic of the church. Three aspects caused the greatest concern to Paul and others who followed his line of teaching in the early church:

1. The question of the Law

The Jewish mind was steeped in the understanding of the Torah — the Law of God. It would be inconceivable for traditional Jews to imagine that the Law had been done away with or superseded in any regard. Consequently the emphasis was made very strongly that Christians, Jews and Gentiles alike, follow the details of the Law, the observance of the rituals, and the fulfilment of the moral requirements. Paul indicated how shortsighted this was.

The question of the Law was the centre of much of Paul's thinking. Was Christianity to be another chamber of the Temple?

Were the Levitical rites, ceremonies, fasts and feasts permanent in God's scheme of things? Or were they serving a purpose which no longer required their fulfilment? The key issue concerning the law lay in the question: Is salvation secured by rites, by initiation, by behaviour; in other words, by what we do? Or is it secured for us by God's grace in action through Christ which is appropriated by our faith?

To Paul the answer was strikingly clear and the alternative extremely dangerous. But to the ordinary Jewish Christian other issues came quickly to mind. 'Did Jesus fulfil the Law of Moses?' 'Did Jesus in his own lifetime pay tax to the Temple, offer sacrifices, keep the fasts and feasts?' 'Was he not circumcised himself?' Some Christians then and since have sought to divide the Law into an inner and an outer, a ceremonial and an ethical, and stress that the Christian is not required to keep the ceremonial and the outer observance but the ethical and inner observance. But even this compromise would not have been acceptable to Paul.

Paul made three things clear:
(a) Our righteousness does not lie in our obedience to the Law. Paul said that we are made right with God, not by anything that we do through a righteousness of our own, but through our faith in what Christ has accomplished for us.[4]
(b) The Law was to bring us to faith in Christ and consequently our allegiance is to the person of Christ not to obedience to the Law, no matter how great or good that might be.

(c) Christ superseded the Law by putting people right through faith. As Paul told the Romans: 'Sin must not be your master; for you do not live under law but under God's grace.'[5]

Even today many Christians do not understand that, and some churches still stress our reliance upon the ten commandments and our obedience to the moral law. Some churches even seek to continue some of the rituals, feasts and fasts of the old covenant, completely failing to realise that Christians live under a new covenant, in spite of the fact that every time they celebrate the Lord's Supper they repeat his words, 'this cup is God's new covenant sealed with my blood, which is poured out for you.'[6] The followers of Herbert W. Armstrong, the Jehovah's Witnesses and the Seventh Day Adventists make this error.

Paul is much clearer than that. Christ was the completion of the Law, he fulfilled the Law, and consequently he terminated the necessity of the Law.

2. The question of circumcision and food laws

At first the question of Gentile converts who became Christians having to be circumcised was not an issue. Cornelius, following the visit of Peter, believed, was baptised, and became a Christian. He was not required to be circumcised. The trouble began in a serious way in Antioch when Paul and Barnabas argued against some Jewish believers who said circumcision was necessary for salvation. As a result, a council of leading Christians was called to meet in Jerusalem. It was not a council of the leaders of all the churches, but of those leaders who were in Jerusalem, that is the more conservative and Jewish of the Christian leaders, and those who came to visit them from Antioch led by Paul.

At this meeting Paul was absolutely forthright. The day was carried, however, by Peter who recounted his own experience of how 'God chose me from among you to preach the Good News to the Gentiles so that they could hear and believe ... He made no difference between us and them; he forgave their sins because they believe. So then, why do you now want to put God to the test by laying a load on the backs of the believers which neither our ancestors nor we ourselves are able to carry? No! We believe and are saved by the grace of the Lord Jesus, just as they are.'[7]

After much debate James summed up the issue by telling them 'not to eat any food that is ritually unclean because it has been offered to idols; to keep themselves from sexual immorality; and not to eat any animal that has been strangled, or any blood.'[8]

In one sense James merely confused the issue. Instead of indicating that not only was circumcision no longer required but neither were any of the other ceremonial or ritual requirements of the Law to be obeyed, he lay down four requirements, three of them having to do with food restrictions as was typical of the legalism of the Jewish upbringing, and the fourth concerning sexual immorality. These requirements, following on a statement that they

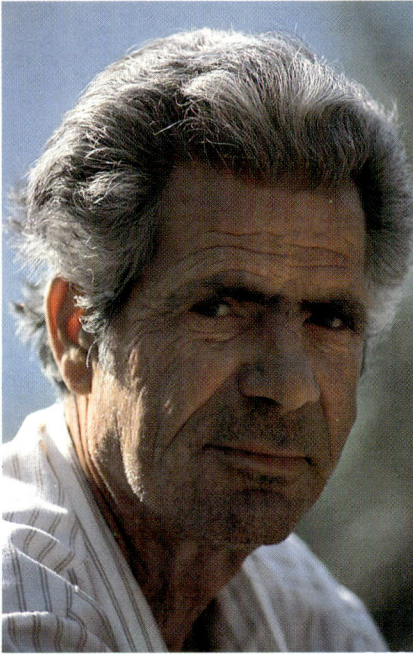

3. The question of legalism

This was a much more difficult issue and one which in the long run was to continue to trouble the church throughout the rest of its life. Paul constantly ran into people who were emphasising the necessity of a legalistic approach to the Christian faith: that Christianity was a list of 'do's and don'ts' and of living a life of obedience to them.

Paul was constantly to emphasise that Christians did not live under this kind of legalistic approach which ultimately led to living a life of misery, under the Law and 'in the flesh'.

Those who lived with a legalistic humanistic attitude lived 'in the flesh'. Ultimately that led to sin and to death. Paul argued strongly for a life lived in the Spirit, which was free from the demands, regulations and restrictions of the Law, and which was lived by the grace of God.

In every century since there

were not required to be circumcised, still made some restrictions on the early Gentiles. These basically practical matters were concessions to make the Gentiles more acceptable to Jews who were meeting with them in their congregations. The council did not come out as clearly as Paul would have desired, but the concessions were minor and acceptable. So Paul remained quiet, having won the major issue.

Paul was a free man: he had no need to keep any laws, either food or ethical laws, provided he lived his whole life under 'the law of Christ' which gave him a higher standard of personal conduct and relationships. Although the question of circumcision had the capacity to divide the early church, it was an issue that soon died out.

have been those who have sought to make Christianity a matter of rules and regulations, of prohibitions and restrictions. Their statements were 'a real Christian wouldn't . . .', 'a true Christian would not wear such clothes or go to the . . .'. Christianity has been in constant danger of being made an exercise in cultural conformity, of decent behaviour. Consequently in different generations, dancing, make-up, theatre attendance, sports, activities on Sunday, hair styles, clothing styles, family outings, music and the like have been forbidden. To be a Christian has meant to obey the social and cultural rules.

But Paul argued strongly that Christianity was neither a matter of our conformity to culture, nor our moral behaviour: it lay in the essence of our faith in what Christ has done for us upon the cross.

The answer that has come back in every generation is that such belief is not enough and it must be accompanied by good behaviour. Of course, the person of belief will carry his belief out in practice. But Paul's fundamental point is absolutely right — that our relationship with God precedes the quality of our behaviour, that faith determines our good works. A Christian is not saved by the good deeds he does, but because he has been saved he must devote his life to good deeds.

The central themes of Paul's apologia

Paul was a unique person in that he contended for his faith with every fibre of his being, yet in so doing promoted not himself, or his cause, but promoted Jesus Christ. There are five central themes in Paul's *apologia*.

1. The love of God

To Paul nothing was more marvellous than the love and grace of God. He did not look upon God as severe, punishing and wrathful, although all of these aspects of his character belonged to his justice. Instead he was a loving Father whose character is perfect, who in love creates, orders and provides for all and who in Jesus makes us right with himself.

'There is for us only one God the Father, who is the creator of all things, and for whom we live.'[9] In every letter that Paul wrote he always called God, Father. There was one God who was the Father and creator of all. The nature of that Father was love. His love was expressed in the way he has cared for us, provided for us and, in Jesus Christ, brought us back to himself.

His character is perfect, and his motive in all of his relationships is love. 'God has shown us how much he loves us — it was while we were still sinners that Christ died for us! By his sacrificial death we are now put right with God.'[10]

2. The uniqueness of Jesus

Except in two letters of Paul (2 Thessalonians and Philemon), each letter stresses the fact that Jesus is the Son of God. Typical of his statements is 'Christ is the visible likeness of the invisible God. He is the first-born Son, superior to all created things. For through him God created everything in heaven and on earth, the seen and the unseen things, including spiritual powers, lords, rulers and authorities. God created the whole universe through him and for him. Christ existed before all things and in union with him all things have their proper place.'[11] His great passage to the Philippians was possibly an early hymn sung in Antioch, but it describes beautifully Paul's concept of the uniqueness of Jesus:

He always had the nature of God,
But he did not think that by force
He should try to become equal with God.

Instead of this, of his own free will,
He gave up all he had,
    And took the nature of a servant.

And became like man,
    And appeared in human likeness.

He was humble and walked the path
Of obedience all the way to death –
    His death upon a cross.

For this reason God raised him to
The highest place above
    And gave him the name that is
    Greater than any other name.

And so, in honour of the name of Jesus
All beings in heaven, on earth
    And in the world below
    Will fall on their knees.

And all will openly proclaim
That Jesus Christ is Lord
To the glory of God the Father.[12]

The life and teaching of Jesus does not occupy a large place in the teaching of Paul. Indeed he seems quite indifferent to the details of what we would normally regard as interesting biography. He mentions nothing of the details concerning the birth of Jesus save that Jesus was born at the most appropriate time. He says nothing of his early life and hardly anything of his teaching.

The death of Jesus upon the cross was the central factor in the teaching of Paul. In letter after letter he proclaimed the significance of the cross. A typical statement is: 'I made up my mind to forget everything except Jesus Christ and especially his death on a cross.'[13] In the death of Jesus Paul saw God's purpose in bringing mankind back to himself. He changed us 'from enemies into his friends and gave us the task of making others his friends also.'[14] Jesus' death upon the cross and his resurrection from it was the central act in the divine drama of human redemption.

The resurrection of Jesus completes what was accomplished upon the cross. God who allowed man's sin to crucify Christ demonstrated his power and love through raising him from the dead. When Paul wrote his first letter to the Christians in Corinth he stressed the significance of the resurrection of Jesus in the mighty fifteenth chapter. The resurrection of Jesus is an act of power by God for our benefit. The most remarkable aspect is not that God raised Jesus from the dead, but that God incorporates our future life through his resurrection, that we too share in the benefits of the resurrection. Paul puts it

succinctly: 'By our baptism, then, we were buried with him and shared his death, in order that, just as Christ was raised from death by the glorious power of the Father, so also we might live a new life.'[15] It was that power that God demonstrated in raising Jesus from the dead that becomes central to the effectiveness of our own living. 'How very great is his power at work in us who believe. This power working in us is the same as the mighty strength which he used when he raised Christ from death and seated him at his right side in the heavenly world.'[16]

The uniqueness of Jesus — in his life and teaching, his death upon the cross, his resurrection and ascension — is all gathered together in Paul's understanding of our relationship with him: we are 'In Christ'. That phrase is the distinctive phrase found in the writings of the apostle Paul. More than two hundred times he uses it throughout his thirteen epistles and in his public speeches. It was the essence of his understanding of what it means to be a Christian. A Christian is one whose life is incorporated into the risen, ascended Lord. From the time we are baptised 'in Christ' our whole Christian experience in life, in death, and beyond death is lived 'in Christ'.

Christianity is never a code of behaviour, or an article of belief; it is a living relationship 'in Christ'. It is Jesus resurrected from the dead and ascended into heaven as Lord; the Messiah as foretold by the prophets is the one in whom our Christian experience exists. That theme was in Paul's *apologia*.

3. Justified by God's grace through faith

Martin Luther described the doctrine of justification by faith as 'the article of faith that decides whether the church is standing or falling'.[17] For Martin Luther justification by faith was the keystone of a church that was true to New Testament doctrine.

For Paul, as for Luther himself, the struggle to be righteous before God was man's ultimate struggle and in our strength it ends in despair and misery. The only righteousness that we can obtain is through the righteousness of Christ.

Paul uses a number of words that describe our relationship with God through our faith.

(a) *Justification* is the means by which we are made right with God through his grace. Fifteen times in Romans and eight times in Galatians, Paul declares that we have been justified or made right with God. Justification is a metaphor which came from the law courts and describes the legal process which has resulted in the guilty being acquitted.

I have complete confidence in the gospel; it is God's power to save all who believe, first the Jews and also the Gentiles. For the gospel reveals how God puts people right with himself: it is through faith from beginning to end. As the scripture says, 'The person who is put right with God through faith shall live'.[18]

Our justification by faith is not salvation by belief, but salvation through the saving righteousness of God through incorporation into Christ Jesus by an active decision of our will, evidenced through our response of faith and baptism.

Justification is God's act of acquitting us of our sin. We are now 'in Christ'.

(b) *Adoption* is a metaphor of our justification that comes from family relationships. Under Roman law an adopted person could pass from one family into another, thus receiving a new father and immediately entering into the family and becoming an heir jointly with the other sons. 'Because of his love God had already decided that through Jesus Christ he would make us his sons — this was his pleasure and purpose.'[19]

His teaching concerning our adoption into the family of God contrasted in its freedom with the spirit of bondage that existed between a slave and his master. We are now no longer slaves, but sons adopted into the family of God.[20]

(c) *Mediation* was the task Jesus undertook following the example of Moses who was the mediator betwen God and Israel, only now he is the mediator between God and mankind. This word which Paul uses comes from the concept of a covenant. As Moses had established the covenant at Sinai, so Christ established a new covenant with himself being the mediator, and his blood being the means by which the new covenant is effected. Only one person in all of history could have established that relationship between us and God. 'For there is one God, and there is one who brings God and mankind together, the man Christ Jesus, who gave himself to redeem all mankind.'[21]

(d) *Expiation*, or as it is sometimes also understood, propitiation, was also used by

Paul to describe the result of our justification. This was the technical term used for the covering of our sin before the eyes of a wrathful God. Although mentioned several times in other passages of scripture, it was only used by Paul on one occasion. Nothing man could do could make God forgive, but God himself makes for our forgiveness. 'God offered Jesus, so that by his death he should become the means by which people's sins are forgiven through their faith in him.'[22] His blood shed for us, at the mercy seat of God, covered over our sin and therefore saved us from the wrath of God which we so justly deserved.

(e) *Redemption* is a theme that Paul delights to use. To redeem means to set free from captivity, or to buy back that which has been pawned. It was used in the slave market and the pawnshop. Captives were ransomed after having been taken prisoner. God had redeemed Israel from Egyptian bondage.

This redemption, sealed at baptism, guaranteed by the giving of the Holy Spirit, will only be complete with the redemption of our whole being and the universe with us at the coming of Christ. 'For we know that up to the present time all of creation groans with pain, like the pain of childbirth. But it is not just creation alone which groans; we who have the Spirit as the first of God's gifts also groan within ourselves as we wait for God to make us his sons and to set our whole being free.'[23]

(f) *Reconciliation* is the result of our redemption. It means that peace has been made between us and God, that we have been brought back to our rightful king after we have rebelled against him. In Romans Paul says: 'Now that we have been put right with God through faith, we have peace with God through our Lord Jesus Christ.'[24] That reconciliation is God's work. God is never reconciled to man but man is reconciled to God and as a result we have peace.

(g) *Sanctification* is the process by which we as saints of God grow in our Christian experience, being 'in Christ' and becoming more like him. We were made complete, holy, when we were made right with God. Once we became a living sacrifice we were an offering to God. At the same time Christ was the sacrifice made on our behalf with the result that we have been made holy. The only sacrifice we make to God is our complete self and even this is made pure and acceptable by the way he has cleansed and redeemed us.

Because we are in him we have already been 'purified from sin; you have been dedicated to God; you have been put right with God by the Lord Jesus Christ and by the Spirit of our God.'[25] Although we have thus been presented before his presence without spot or blemish, there is still a continuing process by which we are still made clean.

We now live a life avoiding those things that would take us back to our old life, and seeking to be perfect even as he is perfect. This has been one of Paul's great themes.

4. Christian life in the Spirit
When God established the church on the Day of Pentecost he gave to it the dynamic which enabled the great commission of Jesus to be implemented throughout the known world.

Jesus had said that he would send his Holy Spirit who would abide with the believers, equip and empower them, bring to their remembrance his teaching, and be the agent through which the people would be convicted, convinced and converted.

It was the presence of the Holy Spirit in the life of Paul that gave him enormous reserves of strength and energy to accomplish his mission. Time and again in all of his writings and speeches he acknowledges the Spirit of God who controls him, directs him and empowers him. Paul even came to the point of declaring with strength that 'whoever rejects this teaching is not rejecting man, but God, who gives you his Holy Spirit.'[26]

Paul developed four particular themes about the Holy Spirit that have enabled Christians ever since to grow in their concepts and understanding of the significance of the Spirit of God.

(a) The Holy Spirit is the *guarantee* of what God has for us. The use of this word was associated usually with money being given in part payment to bind a bargain or to secure an option on a later sale. From that usage Paul developed the concept that God has given us now the Holy Spirit who is the down payment on all the spiritual treasures that God has in store for us. 'It is God himself who has given us the Holy Spirit in our hearts as a guarantee of all that he has in store for us.'[27]

(b) The Holy Spirit is the *seal* that we belong to God. In the early days a seal or a signet was cut from semi-precious stones or gold, with smaller ones being set in rings and larger ones worn on a chain around the neck. This seal, which was unique to the owner, was to authenticate documents and contracts when it was impressed onto the wax which had to be broken to open the document. It conferred ownership and authenticity and in this sense Paul spoke of the Holy Spirit as being God's mark on our lives, the sign that we belonged to him.[28]

(c) The Holy Spirit is a *helper* in our life. Jesus referred to the Holy Spirit as being the one who came alongside of us to help us as a comforter and strengthener. Paul develops that theme and says, 'in the same way the Spirit also comes to help us, weak as we are. For we do not know how we ought to pray; the Spirit himself pleads with God for us in groans that words cannot express.'[29]

(d) It can all be summed up in the emphasis that Paul made that the Holy Spirit is the *source* of all life. It is through the Spirit that we have life in all of the abundance that Jesus has promised. 'If Christ lives in you, the Spirit is life for you because you have been put right with God, even though our bodies are going to die because of sin.'[30]

The early Christians were equipped and enabled to take the message through the world because of the certainty of the in-dwelling presence of the Holy Spirit.

5. The church

Paul had a grand concept of the kingdom of God and that kingdom had to be brought on earth through the church as the means by which God worked and witnessed in the world in this present era. A close examination of all the uses of the word 'church' in Paul's epistles show that he had a growing concept of the church. To Paul the church was never a building; it was never a place where people gathered, but it was the relationship of Christians one to the other. That relationship of Christians could exist in a particular place and at such times Paul would refer to it as 'the church of God which is in Corinth.'[31]

(a) The church is the *body of Christ*. Paul used this analogy frequently to describe the relationship of Christians with each other and with their Lord.

He used the various parts of the body as analogous to the gifts that different Christians possess. The key thought with Paul is that as the body functions as a unity consisting of many individual parts so the church consisting of many parts with different gifts still has a fundamental unity and purpose. There must be co-operation through the different parts of the body and each part must realise it has a significant place within the whole, even though there is a difference in capacity and performance. His key point is 'all of you are in Christ's body, and each one is a part of it.'[32]

(b) The church is *the bride of Christ*. In one of the most beautiful pictures ever mentioned in scripture, Paul uses the analogy of a bride being prepared, cleansed and beautiful for her groom as in a marriage service. So the church is to prepare herself for the coming of Christ. He goes on to say, 'Husbands, love your wives just as Christ loved the church and gave his life for it. He did this to dedicate the church to God by his word, after making it clean by washing it in water, in order to present the church to himself in all its beauty — pure and faultless, without spot or wrinkle or any other imperfection.'[33]

(c) The church is *the household of God*. In this final analogy Paul pictures the people of God belonging to the family of God enjoying his hospitality here on earth and also in heaven. 'So then, you Gentiles are not foreigners or strangers any longer; you are now fellow citizens with God's people and members of the family of God. [Jesus] is the one who holds the whole building together and makes it grow into a sacred temple dedicated to the Lord.'[34] The glory of this is that both Jew and Gentile by faith are incorporated into the family of God, being his household and growing up to a temple of praise to the Lord.

These, then, are the central themes of Paul's apologia. In his debates with philosophers, his arguments with traditional orthodox Jews and his teaching to young Christians, he reiterated again and again the love and grace of God, the uniqueness of Jesus, the fact that we are justified by the grace of God through our faith, that we live in the Spirit and that we belong to the church of Jesus Christ. What great themes!

The contemporary protagonist

Today in every continent there are fearless witnesses to the faith. Unlike Paul they are not being called to fight against the servants of Diana of Ephesus, but against the philosophies, politics and economics of a new world.

There are many faithful believers in gaol who have stood out for their faith, many who have had their rights taken from them because of their Christian witness, and many in right-wing dictatorships and in left-wing communist regimes who have, in our generation, suffered because they have been willing to take the offensive in proclaiming their faith.

In our world, the contemporary ideologies have been influenced by Darwin's evolutionary philosophies, by Freud's psycho-sexual motivation and by Marx's concept of a classless society. These may be the current 'faiths' against which we must defend the truth. But in the affluent West the carnivorous materialism which eats the hearts of people, the empty hedonism that sends people spinning from one pleasure to another, the secular humanist philosophies that create a barren life and syncretistic philosophies that pick and choose parts of Eastern cults and Western religions to satisfy the taste for something new, all need to have the gospel of Jesus Christ expounded clearly.

And the same themes as Paul's *apologia* are to be the themes we must proclaim! Christians are called upon to witness to their faith, not by the power of their intellect or reason, but by the power of the Holy Spirit who is active whenever we are faithfully witnessing to Jesus. God does not need our ability to defend it, but our availability. God does expect us to witness. As Martin Luther said, 'Let us not be anxious; the gospel needs not our help, it is sufficiently strong itself. Our breath need not range against the sophists; what would this bat accomplish by its flappings?'

God does not call us to be pugnacious, litigious or argumentative, but he does expect us to say a good word for Jesus. He expects us to say, like the man at Siloam, 'I was blind, and now I can see.'[35]

For personal reading

Theme: Champion for a cause

MONDAY
Striving for the prize
Philippians 3:7-21

TUESDAY
Salvation through faith not tradition
Romans 4:13-25

WEDNESDAY
Spiritual circumcision
Romans 2:17-29

THURSDAY
Beware of false teachers
2 Corinthians 11: 4-16

FRIDAY
Defection from the truth
Galatians 1:6-12

SATURDAY
Crucified with Christ
Galatians 2:17-21

SUNDAY
We are heirs of the Father
Romans 8:5-17

For group study

Topic: When opposition assails you

1 Paul was a champion for Jesus Christ. Who were some of those who vehemently opposed him and why?

2 Show two examples of how Paul clearly defended his faith in Jesus Christ.

3 What were some of the points of contention between Paul and his opponents? Would there be some parallel arguments by those who oppose Christ's church today?

4 How would you convince another of God's love and of the centrality of Jesus in your faith?

5 The author says that man cannot save himself. We can only be made right with God through his grace. Look again in Romans 3:22-25 and share what this means to you.

6 What can we learn from Paul about being a fearless witness to the faith?

7

Paul the Philosopher

'Have you heard the latest?' We are immediately all ears. We fear being behind someone else in our knowledge. We enjoy being a voyeur on the troubles of another, and we have a desperate hope that in the latest will be something that will give meaning and coherence to our lives.

'What's new?' That question brings us the verbal equivalent of junk mail! Robert Persig said: '"What's new?" is an interesting question but one which results only in an endless tirade of trivia and fashion, the silt of tomorrow. I would like instead to be concerned with the question "What is best?", a question which cuts deeply rather than broadly, a question whose answers tend to move the silt downstream.'

Most of us would do better to turn off the media with the latest news and instead ponder about the meaning of what is happening to us. To think clearly, critically and constructively, to possess a value system based upon past thought, to have a philosophy of life is the highest function of the brain.

All of us have the capacity and the obligation to come to a cohesive understanding of the meaning of life at our own level of competence. This often leads to conflict with others who are doing the same, as Paul found.

A conflict of philosophies

First, Paul had a conflict with some of the *first disciples*. Although Peter, together with James, had already achieved status within the church as apostles, Paul did not hesitate to correct both of them on a matter of dispute concerning the reception of the Gentiles into the church. How good it would have been to have had some letter written by James or Peter giving their side of the events! As it is, we have Paul writing to the Galatians:

But when Peter came to Antioch, I opposed him in public, because he was clearly wrong. Before some men who had been sent by James arrived there, Peter had been eating with the Gentile brothers. But after these men arrived, he drew back and would not eat with the Gentiles because he was afraid of those who were in favour of circumcising them. The other Jewish brothers also started acting like cowards along with Peter; and even Barnabas was swept along by their cowardly action. When I saw that they were not walking a straight path in line with the truth of the gospel, I said to Peter in front of them all, 'You are a Jew, yet you have been living like a Gentile, not like a Jew. How then can you try to force Gentiles to live like Jews?'[1]

Paul was a persuasive arguer and with both James and Peter he carried the argument.

We do not know the rest of the context of the dispute, but it is obvious that the more conservative James and the uncertain Peter were both wanting to hold back the development of the faith among the Gentiles in a way that was not pleasing to Paul because he had seen a great growth of the faith among the Gentile believers.

A second kind of theological and philosophical dispute occurred frequently with people who belonged to *other religions*. Paul debated with the animists, the devotees of various Greek and Roman gods such as in Crete or in Ephesus, and on occasions with magicians. In the case of one of them, Elymas, Paul confronted him: "'You son of the Devil! . . . The Lord's hand will come down on you now; you will be blind and you will not see the light of day for a time." And at once Elymas felt a dark mist cover his eyes, and he walked about trying to find someone to lead him by the hand.'[2]

A third group opposing Paul were the *leaders of Judaism* who were in deep philosophical conflict with Paul. This reaction is typical:

When the Jews saw the crowds they were filled with jealousy; they disputed what Paul was saying and insulted him . . . .[3]

One example of Jewish arguments against Paul is that presented by the lawyer Tertullus before Felix at Caesarea:

'We found this man to be a dangerous nuisance; he starts riots among the Jews all over the world and is a leader of the party of the Nazarenes. He also tried to defile the Temple, and we arrested him. If you question this man, you yourself will be able to learn from him all the things that we are accusing him of.' The Jews joined in the accusation and said that all of this was true.[4]

His philosophy of history, of Jewish theology and of interpretation of the scriptures were totally unacceptable.

A fourth group of people with whom Paul found constant theological conflict were the *Judaisers*. These were Jewish Christians who believed that Jesus was the Messiah and the fulfilment of the Old Testament prophets, but who opposed strongly the introduction of Gentiles within the church. However they believed that Paul was a dangerous radical who was changing the customs handed down from Moses, was a threat to the Temple and denied the traditions of the people. It might be remembered that these were the same charges that led to the stoning of Stephen and the crucifixion of Jesus. The Judaisers were Christian believers who wanted to keep Christianity a sect within Judaism. They followed Paul wherever he went and tried to undercut his teaching and undermine his authority:

Some men came from Judea to Antioch and started teaching the believers, 'You cannot be saved unless you are circumcised as the Law of Moses requires'. Paul and Barnabas got into a fierce argument about this matter.[5]

Paul encountered similar problems in a number of places.

A fifth group with whom Paul had argument and debate were the *philosophers*, usually Greek, who believed that the way of salvation came through wisdom and understanding. Sometimes they were people who, according to Paul, just rationalised their behaviour:

There are many whose lives make them enemies of Christ's death on the cross. They are going to end up in hell, because their god is their bodily desires. They are proud of what they should be ashamed of, and they think only of the things that belong to this world.[6]

Others were like the philosophers in Athens who came from the Epicurean and Stoic schools of philosophy and who debated with Paul, claiming him to be 'this ignorant show-off'.[7] Paul debated with them and proclaimed Jesus and his resurrection before them.

It is to this last group we now turn.

Philosopher on the run

Following the decade of Alexander the Great's conquest (334-323 BC), there spread through the conquered world the benefits of the Golden Age. Greek civilisation, Greek language and Greek philosophy spread through the captured territory and settled with those Greek generals who, after the death of Alexander, ruled the Egyptian, Syrian and Macedonian kingdoms. The Roman conquerors from 31 BC politically dominated the world by their armed might and superior armies, but the Roman world was in turn captured by Greek philosophy. Hellenism, to give it its correct name, conquered the Roman world.

Many early Christians were influenced by Hellenic culture more than by the Jewish culture which gave birth to the Christian faith. In the early church we see the seeds of conflict between the Hellenic and Jewish cultures. Judea was part of the Hellenic world, and in some Jewish synagogues the worship was even conducted in Greek. This conflict of cultures came to a focus in the early church: 'Some time later, as the number of disciples kept growing, there was a quarrel between the Greek-speaking Jews and the native Jews. The Greek-speaking Jews claimed that their widows were being neglected in the daily distribution of funds.'[8] This concern about the inequality of charity resulted in seven deacons being elected to oversee the charitable works of the early church. But the conflict arose because of the favouritism of one culture over another.

The Acropolis: Athens

When the church developed in Antioch and was spread by Paul and others throughout the Gentile world, Hellenic culture began to dominate it. It is in this context that Paul entered Athens, the home of Hellenic culture. By the time of Paul, Greek philosophy was sceptical, humanist and sophisticated. The great Academy of Plato (founded 387 BC) and the Lyceum of Aristotle (founded 335 BC) were in decline as a force in the thought world of the Greeks. Three groups of philosophers were present the day Paul arrived in Athens.

There were the *Epicureans*. They were the followers of Epicurus (342-270 BC) who taught that man was made to achieve noble forms of pleasure, where virtue led to true happiness. However, by the first century much of his teaching had been perverted, particularly by the Romans who followed his teachings to the point of believing that everything that gives pleasure is good. This was hedonism at its clearest. Paul characterised it by quoting to the Christians in nearby Corinth: 'as the saying goes, "Let us eat and drink, for tomorrow we will die".'⁹ The Epicureans believed that gods could exist but if they did they were far removed from this mortal life. They did not believe in immortality, arguing strongly against Platonists, and they thought that the concept of resurrection from the dead was ridiculous.

The second group of philosophers who were present when Paul entered Athens were the *Stoics*. The Stoics were followers of Zeno who in the third century BC lectured in contemporary wisdom. The Stoics lived by acknowledging the priority of reason. Behind everything was the eternal Logos — mind or providence. By subduing passion and disciplining emotion, the Stoic removed himself from the changing fortunes and attitudes of life and sought to align himself with that Logos. Christians emphasised that Jesus was the Logos.¹⁰ To align yourself with the eternal mind behind the universe required not human reason, but acceptance of Jesus and his death and resurrection. Paul came from Tarsus, a noted Stoic-training centre. He knew the classical authors, poets and literature, as is evidenced by his quoting them, though it is unlikely that he was specifically trained in them.

A third group of philosophers who heard Paul in Athens were the believers of the *mystery religions* who followed the teachings and practices either of the religions of the East — Artemis, Serapis, Isis, astrology or the Great Mother — or else they followed the Greek and Roman gods — Dionysus, Orpheus, Zeus or Jupiter. These religions rarely affected a person's behaviour and were regarded by both Greeks and Romans as superstition, closely associated with patriotism, humanism and pantheism. A number of these religions are alluded to in the book of Revelation of John. While these were not in the classical sense philosophies, they did provide for many a philosophy of living, contrary to Christian beliefs. Paul encountered all of these philosophies simultaneously.

Paul in Athens

The capital of modern Greece has been settled continually for 5,000 years. Its great building programmes were begun in the sixth century BC and the greatest of all, the Parthenon, finely designed and executed in the best marble, was completed in 438 BC. The Agora, beneath the Parthenon, was the commercial centre consisting of public buildings and a great plaza where citizens could meet for discussion and philosophical debate. When Paul came into the Agora in Athens to talk about the new Christian faith he knew exactly what he was doing. This was the site for philosophical discussion.

Paul had studied at the university city of Tarsus. He then trained in the key religious centre of Jerusalem. He would die later in the political capital, Rome. But on this day Paul walked into the intellectual capital of the Roman world — Athens.

As he stood in the Agora surrounded by public buildings, marble columns and beautiful temples, and standing on the same spot as Socrates, Plato and the other great philosophers before him, he began to present the Christian philosophy of life before the crowds of Athenians and many philosophers.

There was nothing the Athenians liked more than to hear the latest news. And Paul brought them the good news from God. The Areopagus or 'the Court of Ares' was the judicial advisory council that heard criminal cases. It also had the responsibility of listening to significant presentations of non-legal matters, particularly religious affairs. After Paul had begun preaching about his religious news, he was summoned to appear before this council. He may have appeared at the Royal Porch, where even today the seating cut into the rock can be seen. Whether he was on this site or in the restored stoa nearby cannot be ascertained. But a more noble setting could hardly be imagined for the launching of Christian truth among the intellectuals.

Here is a summary outline of Paul's argument to the Athenians:[11]

(a) God is in the heart of this city
Athens was a very religious place. God, the unknown, is there. Commencing with a reference to a local shrine dedicated to 'an unknown God', Paul then proceeds to build his argument.

This unknown god was the creator of all. God is not confined to idols or temples — as the famous Athenian philosopher, Xenophanes, argued. This God, Paul was declaring, is self-sufficient, not requiring anything from us.

Paul, in placing stress on the fact that God is a spiritual being who is the source of all life, would have gained the support of the Stoics. In his teaching that this God is self-sufficient, he would have gained the support of the Epicureans. Notice that Paul does not use any Old Testament or Hebrew texts. This is because these people did not understand the Jewish law or history. Paul started where the Athenians were, indicating the relevance of the true God to their situation. The people of Athens did not believe in God, had no sense of guilt or sin, and had no awareness of their need of a Saviour. So Paul starts, not with God's answer to mankind's need, but with his audience's fundamental understanding of the nature of God and of his existence.[12]

(b) We are to seek God

Paul now indicates that this unknown God requires us to seek him and find him. Paul argues that we are all one brotherhood and any of us seeking him will find that 'God is actually not far from any one of us'. Paul quotes two Greek poets, Epimenides and Aratus, who in their poetry substantiated these very points. These poets, one from Crete, the other from Cilicia, support his case.[13]

(c) Jesus is our way to God

God wants us to come to him, so he has provided a way. He expects us to turn from our self-centredness, to turn away from our wicked ways and to repent of our sin. Paul quickly comes to the centre of the gospel. Because of our guilt God will judge the whole world through one man whom he has appointed to be our judge and 'has given proof of this to everyone by raising that man from death.'[14]

To this clear-cut outline of Paul's philosophy the listener has only one logical response: to repent of sin and to trust in this risen Jesus, the coming judge.

But at this point of his presentation Paul was interrupted and unable to finish his address. The council broke into debate over the question of the resurrection. Some scoffed at him, thinking he was introducing *two* gods: one called 'Jesus' and the other called 'Resurrection'! Others wanted to hear him speak further and asked him to return. Still others believed, including Dionysius (a member of the council), a woman named Damaris and some other people.[15]

That was in fact quite an incredible response to his philosophical presentation of the gospel. Even to this day, where that speech of Paul's stands inscribed in bronze in the midst of the Areopagus, the only names known from this period of Greek history happen to be the names of the two who believed.

The Athenians wanted their ears tickled with the latest intellectual fad. Paul started at the point of their ignorance. He then brought them new truth about God who was creator, provider and judge, introducing them to Jesus, whom God had raised from death. Through him we have access to God; before him we shall be judged.

Though interrupted, Paul's address is the classic defence of the Christian faith, a practical model for Christian apologetics.

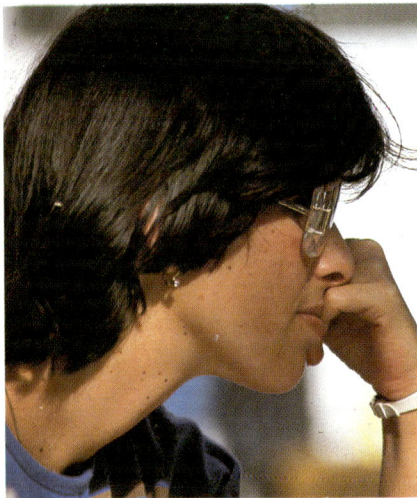

For personal reading

Theme: Christ, the basis of our faith

MONDAY
: Our God needs no sacrifice
Acts 17:16-32

TUESDAY
: The goodness of God
Acts 14:8-18

WEDNESDAY
: We walk in the light
Ephesians 5:1-14

THURSDAY
: Reconciled to Christ
Colossians 1:21-29

FRIDAY
: Paul's philosophy opposed
Acts 13:44-52

SATURDAY
: Worldliness condemned
Philippians 3:17-21 and 1 Corinthians 15:28-34

SUNDAY
: The body of Christ
Ephesians 4:1-16

For group study

Topic: Thinking through the meaning of life

1 Today we hear many claims and many voices. Each one demands our attention. How can we tell right from wrong? What should be the basis of our faith?

2 Read again John 1:1-3, and 14. What is that promise regarding the centrality of Jesus as the word? How does it strengthen your faith?

3 Examine again Paul's three main theses from Acts 17:16-34:
(a) God is a spiritual being who is the source of all life. Do we believe in the living, vital presence of God in daily life?
(b) God has made it possible for us to find him. Do we really seek God?
(c) Jesus is our only way to God. In practical terms what does it mean to give ourselves to him? Why is it only possible to discover God as he really is through Jesus? Compare Colossians 1:15, 19-20; and Romans 3:23-26.

8

Paul the Patriot

On the edge of the western shore of the Dead Sea, the lowest point of the earth's surface, is a remarkable sight. As the sun rises in the dry desert air, light captures the top of a rock 1,300 feet high. At this spot in AD 70 , Masada earned a place in history.

Jewish revolt had been smouldering for seven years against the Romans. After four years the Roman General Titus conquered Jerusalem, destroyed the Temple, massacred the citizens and completely demolished the city with the stones being dumped over the city walls into the valley below. A remnant of Jewish rebels held a former holiday fort of King Herod the Great against the might of the Roman Empire.

Stocked with food and water, the rebels held out for three years against the Roman army until the Roman governor built a huge ramp which enabled the Romans to destroy the walls. Rather than lose their liberty, the 960 Jews decided to commit suicide, thus robbing the Romans of the fruits of victory and providing a rich heritage of courage for the Jewish race. Today at Masada members of the Jewish armoured guard shout 'Masada shall not fall again!' That shout of pride and fierce determination represents, graphically, Jewish patriotism.[1]

Jewish issues today

It is possible to meet in Israel Jews by birth, by religion and by citizenship. The equation becomes more difficult when some are not Jews by birth or religion but are by citizenship, while others are not Jews by birth or citizenship but are by religion. Still others are not Jews by religion or citizenship but are by birth! It is very difficult to identify a Jew, particularly as so many have the racial characteristics of a score of races and yet twelve million people identify themselves as 'Jewish'. As one scholar said, 'He is a Jew who says he is'. Normally a person is accepted as a Jew if his mother is a Jew.

Four contemporary issues concern those who care for the Jewish people and their religion. The first was the *Holocaust*, that incredible programme of genocide perpetrated by the Nazis in World War II. The impact of the Holocaust was horrendous upon the families of Israel. Wherever Jews gather around the world, the Holocaust unites them with a feeling of bitterness and national suffering.

Second, *anti-semitism*. In the Christian era, anti-Jewish feeling first occurred in the fourth century AD when the Roman Emperor became Christian; then again it appeared in the middle ages when the Germanic kingdom of the Franks sought to protect Europe from Islam and began a religiously based anti-semitism. There were other tragic occurrences in Europe, culminating in Adolf Hitler who persecuted Jews and Christians alike. Jewish political philosopher, Hannah Arendt, has indicated that whenever there is a suppression of true spiritual Christianity, anti-semitism is one of the results. Whenever Christians have been spiritual and close to Christ, such as were the Wesleyans, the Pietists and evangelicals of our era, they have been friends and supporters of the Jews.

But Christians recognise with shame that over the years many have despised and persecuted the Jews. They would sometimes justify it by referring to those Jews who yelled for the crucifixion of Jesus: 'Let the responsibility for his death fall on us and on our children'.[2] Roman Catholics, at the time of the Inquisition in Spain, enforced conversion at the point of a sword. Martin Luther spoke foully of the Jews. Shakespeare presented an indelible caricature of Jews with the moneylender Shylock, and today right-wing organisations like the Ku Klux Klan and other extremist groups have continued that anti-semitism.

One Jew has written: 'I don't remember too much about those early years of my life, but I do remember when I was called a "Christ killer" for the first time. I couldn't have been any more than five or six. I rushed home crying, not because I understood what a "Christ killer" was, but because I was afraid of the hate I heard in the voice. Later, when I was eight, I was playing ball in the school yard on a Sunday in July. All I had on was a pair of shorts and my sneakers. As I started home for lunch, I encountered a big, grim-faced woman coming down the street. She stepped directly in my path and with the side of her right arm shoved me across my chest and knocked me down, saying, "Out of my way, ya little kike!" Again that anger — that hate which I could not understand. And I began to cry. I rushed home to my mother, and she quieted me and soothed my tears. That's when Mom started to tell me about what it was like to grow up in the ghetto and about the hatred that the Gentiles had for Jews.'[3]

Third, *Zionism*, a term for the movement to establish the state of Israel. It came into focus in 1896. The original concept was that the Israelis were to occupy Palestine along with the Palestinians who had lived there for centuries. Israel's poor treatment of the Jordanians and the Palestinians in Israel and the surrounding Arab nations has caused much Christian support for Israel to be subdued. The revival of a successful Jewish state has brought great solidarity among the Jewish people. There are 125 references in the Old Testament dealing with the promise of the return of the land. Since 1948, Israel has had its own land and, in the triumphant wars, has stubbornly held that 'this land is my land'.

Christians should not necessarily accept all that Israel does politically and militarily.

Zionism isn't just a fulfilment of scripture; it is a humanist ideology that even atheist Jews can hold. It is a political and nationalistic phenomenon which is not necessarily carrying out the prophecies of the scriptures. Christians also must have a concern for the Palestinian people who inhabited the land before the Israelis, especially for those today who suffer in that part of the world.

The fourth aspect is *messianic Judaism*. There are increasing numbers of Jews who seek to live a consistent Jewish life while being Christian believers. Christian Jews who worship Jesus as the Messiah have been growing in numbers and significance in the

Grave of Theodore Herzl (founder of modern Zionism): Jerusalem

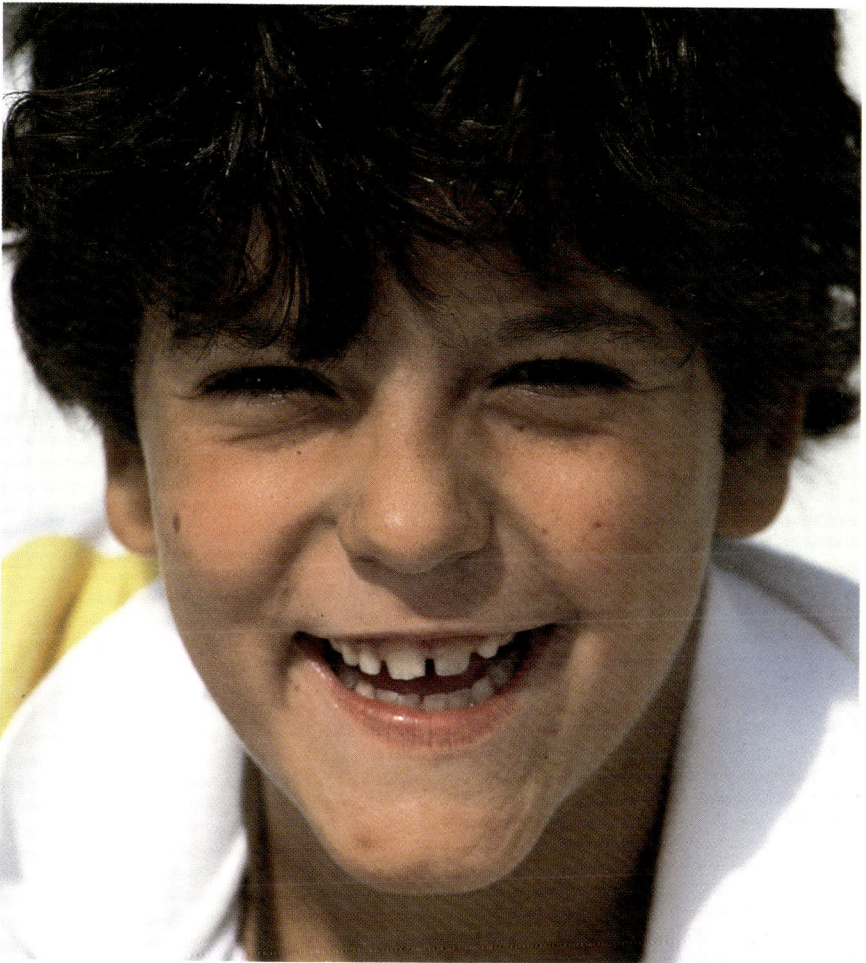

last two decades. They worship the Lord, hold to the centrality of the Torah in worship, celebrate the Passover and the Feast of Tabernacles, keep the Sabbath, keep the traditions, heritage and culture of their people, celebrate Bar Mitzvah, and in every way are fulfilled Jews while still accepting Jesus as the Messiah. It is calculated that more Jews have become Christians as messianic Jews in the past two decades than in the past 2,000 years.

In a world where Jews themselves are questioning what it means to be a Jew, we must ask afresh: 'What is the Christian attitude towards the Jewish people?'

The apostle Paul agonised over his own people. He was a Jew — proud of his race, a patriot who clung to his Jewish traditions. Yet more than anything else, Paul wanted his countrymen to be fulfilled by accepting Jesus as Messiah.

Paul's Jewish heritage

Paul was conscious of the importance of his heritage: 'I was circumcised when I was a week old. I am an Israelite by birth, of the tribe of Benjamin, a pure-blooded Hebrew. As far as keeping the Jewish Law is concerned, I was a Pharisee, and I was so zealous that I persecuted the church. As far as a person can be righteous by obeying the commands of the Law, I was without fault.'[4]

From a child he had learnt how God had chosen his people and initiated a series of covenants with Noah, with Abraham, with Isaac, Jacob and above all with Moses. To Moses the covenants were ratified, promises exchanged and blessings given. Those covenants were renewed at every period of Jewish history and the Jews were proud of their special relationship with, and privileges from, God. In spite of the fact that for centuries they were subject to harsh domination by other nations, at the centre of their life was the sacred law or Torah which held them together even when they were a scattered people. For more than six hundred years before the time of Jesus there had been more Jews living outside of Palestine than inside it, but the one thing that kept them together in national destiny and identity was their commitment as a people to the Law. Paul was proud to stand in this tradition.

There were many advantages in being a Jew even though, because they had rejected Jesus as the Messiah, Paul felt deeply that they had made the gravest error possible.

How great is my sorrow, how endless the pain in my heart for my people, my own flesh and blood! For their sake I could wish that I myself were under God's curse and separated from Christ. They are God's people; he made them his sons and revealed his glory to them; he made his covenants with them and gave them the Law; they have the true worship; they have received God's promises; they are descended from the famous Hebrew ancestors; and Christ, as a human being, belongs to their race. [5]

How proud he was of his own people. But they had rejected Christ. They had refused to see him as the Messiah, the one who would redeem Israel. Now the good news was to be taken to people who were not Jews and, through those who did not belong to his race, the peoples of the earth would be blessed through faith in Christ.

Paul pictures this in an extended allegory found in Romans 9-11. Archeologists have discovered a Roman synagogue which would probably have been known to the Roman Christians, called the 'Synagogue of the Olive'.

Paul likens the people of Israel to a grand old olive tree: 'and if the roots of a tree are offered to God, the branches are his also. Some of the branches of the cultivated olive tree have been broken off.'[6] The Jews of faith who believe in Jesus Christ are still the living branches whose roots and tradition go down into the soil of their faith. But those who have rejected Jesus, who do not believe him to be the Messiah, are broken off and discarded, while some wild olive branches are grafted back into the main trunk of the olive tree. It was a Roman practice to bring new vitality to a tree by placing wild olive branches into the old root. Into the traditions and culture of the people of Israel — the old olive stock — God has implanted new stems of strong virile faith. Those old stems that ceased to have faith have been rejected and broken off. But the miracle is that, although the olive tree now grows with fresh virility, the day will come when the broken-off branches will be restored to their own tree again.

Paul says:

You Gentiles are like that wild olive tree, and now you share the strong spiritual life of the Jews. So then, you must not despise those who were broken off like branches. How can you be proud? You are just a branch: you don't support the roots — the roots support you . . . You Gentiles are like the branch of a wild olive tree that is broken off and then, contrary to nature, is joined to a cultivated olive tree. The Jews are like this cultivated tree; and it will be much easier for God to join these broken-off branches to their own tree again.[7]

Consequently, Paul preached first to his own people. Even though Paul was proud to boast that he was specially called to take the gospel to the Gentiles, he believed the gospel went to 'first the Jews and also the Gentiles'.[8] Thus, after taking the message to his own people first, and being rejected, he would then take it on to others.

On one occasion, Paul and his companions went first to the synagogue at Antioch in Pisidia and gave a message about the nature of salvation, demonstrated through the history of their people. It was only when his message was rejected that:

Paul and Barnabas spoke out even more boldly: 'It was necessary that the word of God should be spoken first to you. But since you reject it and do not consider yourselves worthy of eternal life, we will leave you and go to the Gentiles. For this is the commandment that the Lord has given us: "I have made you a light for the Gentiles, so that all the world may be saved." '[9]

Three times in his letter to the Romans Paul indicates that the Jews come first. They come first in hearing the gospel of salvation,[10] they come first in receiving the wrath of God if they reject the offer of salvation,[11] and they can come first when God gives 'glory, honour and peace to all who do what is good, to the Jews first and also to the Gentiles.'[12] More than anything else the apostle Paul wanted his own people to believe in Jesus as Messiah. He wanted to establish messianic synagogues and congregations of believing Christians.

Jewish rejection of the Messiah and the church

Many Jews, both in Paul's day and since, rejected Jesus as Messiah. They could not comprehend that a carpenter from Nazareth without any formal training — a man of patience and peace, who rejected all of the honours and power of this world, and who had been crucified as a common criminal — could possibly be the Messiah.

Then as now some Jews believed that the Messiah was yet to come, while others believed not in a personal Messiah but in the coming of the messianic era. Still others rejected the concept of a physical redeemer altogether. Jesus had never anticipated that the Jews would accept him as

Messiah. In one of his most moving parables he told how the tenants of a vineyard constantly killed the servants of the owner until the owner sent his own son, but he in turn was taken and thrown out of the vineyard and killed. This was a direct prophecy of what would happen to him. Then Jesus indicated that it was the rejected stone thought worthless by the people that was used by God as the foundation in the kingdom.[13]

The Old Testament has more than three hundred references to the Messiah which can be shown to have been fulfilled in Jesus Christ. There are more than sixty major prophecies which are fulfilled in him and in him alone.

But the church, the body of

believers, was also rejected. Not only in our generation do Jews reject Christians as the true people of God, but in Paul's day the believers were also rejected. This was because the earliest believers were nobodies, mere fishermen, farmers and tax collectors with no training or experience, simply '... ordinary men of no education. They recognised then that they had been companions of Jesus.'[14] They were rejected because of the way they spoke of Christ as Messiah.

Why was this teaching such a particular offence? For two reasons. First, Jesus claimed to be one with the Father — to be God. This struck at the very heart of Jewish monotheism — the idea that God is one and indivisible. Talk of Jesus as 'God's Son' suggested to orthodox Jews that Christians were claiming there were two gods! This was a logical

impossibility as well as rank heresy. Second, the Jews did not believe that a crucified person could be under the blessing of God. Instead their Law taught: 'If a man has been put to death for a crime and his body is hung on a post, it is not to remain there overnight. It must be buried the same day, because a dead body hanging on a post brings God's curse on the land.'[15] Henceforth a crucified Saviour was an enormous stumbling block, though the early Christians used this as the key point in their proclamation of the gospel. Jesus took upon himself the curse of the Law in order that we might be freed from the Law's curse ourselves.

When his people rejected both his Saviour and his brothers in Christ, Paul felt constantly ostracised. He still took the message to his own people, but he proclaimed that the Temple was no longer necessary, that Jewish customs could be changed, that the Law and ritual were now fulfilled in Christ, that now the day of the resurrection of Jesus was the new Lord's Day, that circumcision of the flesh was not required, only circumcision of the heart, to be a true Jew.

It can easily be seen why his own people rejected Paul. Paul gave three pointers which help us understand God's attitude to Jewish rejection of Jesus:
(a) God gave his people a free choice
Paul believed the Jews were the chosen people of God: they were given all the privileges attached to this, yet they rejected Jesus as Messiah. God never forces people against their own will. He respects their right to choose, even when that choice is conspicuously wrong.
(b) The Jews were responsible for their own choice
God did not make them reject Jesus. They of all people should have had faith, but they refused to believe. Paul's attitude to his fellow Jews is shown when he says: 'My brothers, how I wish with all my heart that my own people might be saved! . . . They have not known the way in which God puts people right with himself, but instead, they have tried to set up their own way; and so they did not submit themselves to God's way of putting people right.'[16] That disobedience and refusal to believe is why the Jews placed themselves outside the salvation of God.
(c) Yet God still loves the Jews and will give them a chance to be saved
That is the wonderful grace of God. God still has faithful believers among his chosen people. Paul believed that there was a remnant of Israel who were still able to respond in faith.[17] There will still be great rejoicing because both Gentile and Jew will be one in their commitment to God through faith in Christ.

Some commentators believe that Paul has allowed his patriotism to run away with his theology. They say that because the Jews have rejected Christ they have no more special place in the economy of God than any others who have rejected him. But Paul's teaching is clear: there is still a special place in the heart of God for the people he called his own; one day they will be reunited with the whole family of God.

The Christian attitude to Jews

In a world where one race of people have been disproportionately disadvantaged, prejudiced and rejected over the centuries, Christians must have a very clear understanding of their response to Jewish people.

☐ Christians should have a high regard for Jews as God's chosen people.

☐ We should support the rights of natural justice for Jews and be strongly opposed to any anti-semitism as racist and objectionable. The Christian should reject jokes, snide business stories, stereotypes and caricatures of Jews.

☐ We must remember that it was from the Jewish race that Jesus, and therefore salvation, came — and be grateful.

☐ God still has a purpose for the Jews connected with the future purposes of the coming of the Messiah. The scripture states that all Israel will yet be saved. Although there are no clear details of when and how this will happen, Christians believe it.

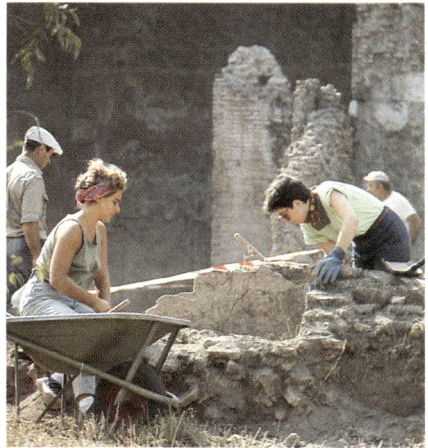

☐ Christians should co-operate with Jews in all kinds of community work and social endeavour. We both have the same background of love for God the Father, the ten commandments and the standards of behaviour that come from a Judeo-Christian tradition. We have a common heritage of behaviour and belief that links us together beyond what humanist and secularist people can understand.

☐ We should help our Jewish friends to hear our own witness that Jesus is the Messiah, and that they can only be fulfilled as Jews by understanding and believing in him.

Some Christians want to show their respect for Jews and therefore will not discuss Christian matters with them, nor present to them Christ as Messiah. That is really a form of anti-semitism in that it discriminates against Jews by preventing them discovering Jesus as Israel's promised Messiah. Christians have a responsibility to evangelise the Jews but in love with understanding.

The gospel is clear. All of us, Jew and Gentile alike, have sinned, but we are all able to be saved through Jesus the Messiah.

The American Jewish author, Stan Telchin, has the final word:

How shall we believers deal with each other? Paul summed it up in the first chapter of Ephesians: 'The Messiah came to the Gentiles as well as the Jews to reconcile them both to God the Father; each of them has been selected and adopted into God's family in exactly the same way: each of them is a joint heir with Jesus and, therefore, they are joint heirs with one another.'

As a result of all my months of study, prayer and experience, I came to this position.

I am a Jew, I was born a Jew, and I will die a Jew. Even if it were possible for me to reject my Jewish identity and heritage, I would never do so. I am a Jew by birth and by desire.

As a Jew, I am even more sensitive to the teachings of Jesus, who was born a Jew, lived as a Jew, chose other Jews as his disciples and loved the Jewish people. As his disciple today, I know that he is more concerned about the attitudes of our hearts than of the actions we perform. This knowledge permits me to have the peace I need to lay all of these issues before him, to cast my cares upon him as I yield to the very Spirit of God and follow after peace, love and joy.

In my relations with other believers, Jews or Gentiles, I am to follow after the peace that passes understanding as I seek the wisdom which comes from above. I am to avoid wrath and anger and striving on my own as the loving nature of God becomes more manifest in me.

In my relations with members of my family and friends I am to remain consistent, never turning my back on my heritage, on my ancestry, on Israel or upon them.[18]

For personal reading

Theme: Patriotism for God's Kingdom

MONDAY	God's plan in history *Acts 13:44-52*
TUESDAY	A great heritage *Acts 24:10-21*
WEDNESDAY	Christ alone counts *Philippians 3:1-11*
THURSDAY	God is impartial *Romans 2:1-16*
FRIDAY	Doers of the law *Romans 2:12-29*
SATURDAY	God's mercy *Romans 9:1-14*
SUNDAY	Confessing and believing *Romans 10:1-10*

For group study

Topic: A message and mission to Jews

1 Paul was a Jew and he was proud of his race. What is the Christian attitude towards Jews?

2 The author mentions Paul's idea of Israel as a grand old olive tree. What truths do you see in this? How does this relate to Christian missions today?

3 How far should religious laws, rules and regulations dictate your lifestyle?

4 What do you understand to be the basis of the Jews' rejection of Jesus as Messiah?

5 Discuss the recommendations of the author on the Christian's attitude to Jews. In what specific ways can these be applied today?

9

Paul the Proclaimer

Proclamation has always accompanied God's message. Throughout the Old Testament it was expected that the believer would speak up for his faith. One example of many is 'Proclaim the greatness of the strong God who saves me!'[1] Jesus called his followers to 'go and proclaim the kingdom of God.'[2] The early church took the proclamation of the kingdom to heart. 'They were all filled with the Holy Spirit and began to proclaim God's message with boldness.'[3]

The importance Paul placed on proclamation is shown in these words to the church at Corinth: 'We proclaim the crucified Christ, a message that is offensive to the Jews and nonsense to the Gentiles, but for those whom God has called, both Jews and Gentiles, this message is Christ, who is the power of God and the wisdom of God.'[4]

Paul had a capacity to proclaim this to a range of people: high Roman officials, governors, perhaps even Caesar himself, Jewish kings, high priests, members of the council of the Sanhedrin, Greek philosophers and members of the council of the Areopagus, superstitious farmers on Malta, the dilettanti of Athens and the credulous peasants of Derbe. Each person he confronted he saw alike: a sinner lost from God who needed the redemption that Christ could bring.

Paul took every opportunity to proclaim the truth about how God had made him a new person. His proclamation was powerful and the evidence of his changed life spoke as eloquently as the words he used.

Paul as orator

Paul quotes the following criticism of himself by the Greeks at Corinth: 'Someone will say "Paul's letters are severe and strong, but when he is with us in person, he is weak, and his words are nothing".'[5] Because Paul refused to be part of the traditional, rational dialectic, they regarded his capacity as a speaker as very limited. He was not a rhetorician in the classical Greek sense. As Paul said:

[Christ] sent me to tell the Good News, and to tell it without using the language of human wisdom, in order to make sure that Christ's death on the cross is not robbed of its power . . . When I came to you, my brothers, to preach God's secret truth, I did not use big words and great learning. . . . my teaching and message were not delivered with skilful words of human wisdom, but with convincing proof of the power of God's Spirit.[6]

However, Paul used all the variety available to a public speaker to present his message forcefully. Michael Green says, 'Paul can spread the good news of it, teach it, announce it, chatter it, make it known or put it forward for discussion.'[7]

Paul's speeches are of three kinds. The first is that of gospel proclamation and includes preaching the good news to the Jews at Antioch, and to the Gentiles, ranging from ignorant peasants at Lystra to educated philosophers at Athens. The second kind of address is the pastoral charge given to the Christian elders of the church at Ephesus when they came and met Paul at Miletus. The third kind of address is his apologetic defence before a rioting mob from Fort Antonia, before the council of the Sanhedrin in Jerusalem, before Jews in Rome, before the Roman Governors, Felix and Festus, and before the Jewish king at Caesarea.

Paul took every opportunity to speak a good word for Jesus. Sometimes he spoke formally as in the synagogue, but mostly he spoke informally with people about him. He discussed, debated, argued, disputed, and witnessed — all different words used in the Acts to describe his proclamation.

He was also a courageous opportunist in speaking about Jesus: in a storm at sea, in the ruins following an earthquake, in prison, in a public hall, in the midst of a local religious festival, before the city authorities, and while being rescued from a lynch mob! Any time, anywhere, with anyone — that was the basis of his proclamation.

In his presentation Paul could be polemical: he could dispute, argue and debate. The speeches of Paul found in the latter half of the Acts of the Apostles argue the case for the reality of the resurrected Christ.

His presentation could be quite passionate: 'I have told you this many times before, and now I repeat it with tears: there are many whose lives make them enemies of Christ's death on the cross. They are going to end up in hell.'[8]

Sometimes his address was quite philosophical. He showed in his preaching the grand sweep of history, either the history of the Jews, or of the Gentiles from the time of creation. His addresses in the synagogue at Antioch in Pisidia, and to the philosophers in Athens are classic examples of the variety of his approach.

Paul also was most persuasive: 'From morning till night he explained to them his message about the kingdom of God, and he tried to convince them about Jesus by quoting from the Law of Moses and the writings of the prophets. Some of them were convinced by his words, but others would not believe.'[9]

Paul as author

We usually judge a man as an author by his carefully prepared statements, books written and rewritten, so as to express precisely what he has in mind. But Paul was an author writing out of the immediate situation where he found himself, and in answer to messages and letters about local pragmatic problems. That is how we must judge him: as a writer on the go. His writing was not the work of a systematic theologian or a contemplative thinker. His responses were not written out of careful studies of his previous utterances, or to codify his response in the light of the logic of earlier statements. Note how to the church at Corinth he catches up the pastoral themes: 'Now, to deal with the matters you wrote about. A man does well not to marry'; 'Now, concerning what you wrote about food offered to idols.'[10]

1. Principal epistles

These epistles are those major letters in which Paul expounds his Christian doctrines and understanding. The first, the letter to the Galatians, was probably written about AD 48 . Then followed shortly afterwards, during his second missionary journey, the letters to the Thessalonians which were written while he was in Corinth during the time when Gallio was proconsul there (AD 50-52). His three letters to the church at Corinth, one of which is only a fragment, were written during his longest ministry in any one place, at Ephesus between AD 52 and 55 . The following year, AD 56-57, he wrote the letter to the Romans, either from Ephesus or during his later visit to Corinth.

The Epistle to the Galatians was written to a group of churches that extended from the coast up into the mountains and plains of central Turkey. Paul travelled through this area and founded churches in the southern area — Antioch, Iconium, Lystra and Derbe — during his first missionary journey and subsequently made two further visits. These later visits may have been to churches in the northern area of Galatia as some theologians have cogently argued.

His establishment of the churches in this area was followed up by a group of Judaisers who insisted that the Gentiles must be circumcised and observe the Jewish Law if they were to be saved. Paul was furious that these 'dogs' were snapping at the heels of the new Christians, his doctrine of salvation by faith being turned into a doctrine of salvation through man's obedience and works. Consequently he outlined the doctrine which a year later was to be ratified when the council of Jerusalem convened.

The Epistles to the Thessalonians: Salonica today is a thriving town in Macedonia and over the years has always maintained a Christian witness. Paul came here after his first visit to Philippi, following the call to come to Macedonia. He founded the church in about AD 50. Unfortunately, some of the local Jews stirred up trouble with the Christians who were meeting in Jason's house. Paul sent Timothy back to Thessalonica from Athens to give oversight to the work, and by the time Timothy returned to let him know what was happening, Paul had gone on to Corinth.

His letter to them from Corinth is a letter of joy and teaching on specific issues that had been raised during Timothy's visit. Paul recalls with pleasure his visit to them and the events that occurred after he had left them. He gave teaching on sexual behaviour for Christians, Christian love, the necessity for Christians to be engaged in work, on Jesus' return and other matters of Christian behaviour. However, this letter itself caused some misunderstanding, particularly over the imminence of Christ's return, and so Paul wrote a second letter shortly afterwards giving more definite teaching.

First and Second Corinthians: Paul was staying at Ephesus. A delegation arrived from the Corinthian church giving him reports and seeking his advice on a range of questions. Paul wrote back to them concerning such matters as divisions within the church; court cases between some members; and drunkenness, noise and disorder in the church services during the celebration of the Lord's Supper. He answered questions about marriage, food given to idols, behaviour of women in public meeting places, spiritual gifts and the nature of the body which we possess after death. He followed this letter with another which today does not exist. Some scholars believe a portion of this letter has been included by later copyists in Second Corinthians.

In the meantime, the condition within the church was so bad that Paul paid a second visit to the church which was a most unpleasant experience and he decided not to visit them again. He was still concerned and anxious about what was happening, and was greatly relieved when Titus reached him with news that his second letter (the lost one) had brought the Corinthians to their senses. Paul told the Corinthians that even though that letter caused them so much anguish, it was necessary because they had been wrong and needed correction. His third letter, known as 'Second Corinthians', is therefore a happier one, looking forward to his third visit. It is the most personal of his letters.

The Epistle to the Romans is the greatest of all his letters. Some scholars argue it was written while in Ephesus, others that it was while in Corinth. After taking an offering for the poor of Jerusalem back to Israel, he planned to go west again to Rome, to spend some time with the Christians there, and then be helped by them to continue his missionary journeys on to Spain.

This was the most carefully constructed and argued of his letters and comes closest to a systematic theology. His theme is that for all, both Jew and Gentile, salvation and righteousness is obtained only by faith in Christ. None of us stands guiltless before God for the state of the world. But God offers us new life and peace with himself through our faith in Jesus Christ. This salvation is in line with a true understanding of the nature of faith as expressed by the great Old Testament fathers, and that faith alters every aspect of our lives.

2. Prison epistles
This title covers the letters Paul wrote to the churches at Colossae, Ephesus, Philippi and to Philemon while in prison at Ephesus, Caesarea or Rome, a point disputed by scholars.

The Epistle to the Colossians was sent to the church settled in the Lycus Valley, a hundred miles inland from Ephesus in about AD 61. Two of the men at Colossae became well known in the early church — Philemon, to whom the brief letter was written, and Epaphras, who travelled with Paul and was active in spreading the Christian gospel in their area. Paul had not visited Colossae, but in prison he heard of their faith and wrote to encourage them. It was believed to have been carried as Tychicus was returning to the church at Colossae, accompanied by Philemon's runaway slave Onesimus.
The great theme of the letter to the church at Colossae was the uniqueness of Jesus. The Colossians lived in an area where

many other religions and faiths tried to adapt Christian teaching to their own point of view. Paul indicates the supremacy of Jesus Christ over all other systems and religions.
The Epistle to the Philippians. This church which had stood beside Paul from the first time he set foot in Europe, was founded by him during his second missionary journey between AD 49 and 52 . Luke, who travelled with him, stayed behind to help the church develop and his account in Acts is most favourable. That church continued to send Paul physical aid, money, support and encouragement while he was in prison. The letter is full of joy and peace with strong emphasis upon the quality of the Christian life and faith. It includes the great hymn about Christ's humility and greatness.

The Epistle to Philemon is the shortest of the epistles. It is the only private letter among the writings of Paul and it concerned one specific problem. Philemon was a man of some wealth and status who had been responsible for extending the Christian faith in Colossae. One of his slaves had taken money and escaped. Paul met him during his imprisonment and Onesimus (literally translated as 'useful') had become a Christian. Paul now sends him back home to his master but indicates that as they are both Christians together they are now brothers in Christ. The letter indicates that whatever is owed by Onesimus, Philemon should put it down to Paul's account. It is a letter of tact and praise, of warmth and Christian concern.

The Epistle to the Ephesians:
This one is the most difficult of
the letters to ascribe to Paul. It is
very strange that to the very
centre where Paul had spent his
longest period of ministry there
are no personal greetings, and
even the words 'at Ephesus'[11] are
missing from some manuscripts.
This letter was probably written
to a group of churches in an area
that included some which Paul
had not visited personally. He
thought there were many
opportunities for witness, but also
many adversaries, hardships and
trials through plots of the Jews.
He was also imprisoned here.

The letter rejoices in the
breaking down of the barriers
between Jew and Gentile, stresses
the new unity that is found in
Christ, and outlines the new life
and relationships that the
Christian must have in marriage,
in family life, in relationships
with slaves and employees, and
with the wider community.

3. Pastoral epistles

These three epistles, two to the
young minister Timothy and one
to Titus, grew out of a deep
concern for those who had the
responsibilities of carrying on the
faith. Much of the content of
these pastoral epistles seems to
have been written by Paul, but
most scholars believe they are in
part at least written by other
Christians later. They are
addressed not to churches but to a
special functional class within the
church, perhaps at the time of the
first of the professional ministers.
There are some personal sections
from Paul's life and matters are
written in the spirit of Paul,
possibly to provide the teaching

with authority.

These letters were written out
of Paul's personal concern for
people whom he loved. Words
tumble out over each other and
frequently Paul takes a phrase
that means much to him and out
of that pours one of the most
beautiful of his passages. Chapters
like Romans 8, 1 Corinthians 13,
Philippians 2 and Colossians 1 are
some of the greatest writings in all
of history.

While Paul wrote out of
matters of local concern, the Holy
Spirit gave his words enduring
meaning and a breadth far
beyond his understanding.
Wherever they have been read,
his epistles have been the means
of converting people and changing
the course of history. His Letter to
the Romans alone had a profound
effect upon some of the greatest
thinkers of all time including
Augustine, Luther, Bunyan,
Wesley and Barth.

Paul as encourager

Paul needed many helpers or
'yokefellows' who were able to
shoulder the burden of ministry
with him. Among his co-workers
were Priscilla, Aquilla,
Andronicus, Junius, Aristarchus,
Mark, Justus, Timothy, Titus,
Epaphras, Luke and Demas. From
the time of his first missionary
journey which began with a
companion apostle, Barnabas, and
an assistant, John Mark, Paul
always developed a team
approach to ministry. It is
possible to list some forty persons
who were actual helpers and
sponsors of his activities, and his
letters abound with thanks for the
support that came to him from
these people.

Ephesus

It is interesting to see how Paul speaks about these helpers as this gives us an indication of his capacity to encourage those who worked alongside him.

One clear example of the way Paul uses encouragement is the way he wrote about Epaphroditus. Epaphroditus brought a gift from the church at Philippi while Paul was in prison, but he himself was also a gift from them to stay with Paul and help him. However, he became ill, a real concern and worry to Paul, and so Paul sent him back to the church. But in case the people of Philippi thought that Epaphroditus had failed in his responsibility, he speaks in glowing terms of the contribution Epaphroditus had made to the ministry. He had been 'our brother . . . who has worked and fought by my side . . . who has served as your messenger in helping me . . . as a brother in the Lord. Show respect to all such people as he, because he risked his life and nearly died for the sake of the work of Christ.'[12] Paul used a number of words of Epaphroditus and also of others, all of which are translated by the Greek word *sunergos* which is variously translated as fellow believer, fellow labourer, fellow worker, fellow soldier, fellow partner, fellow passenger. No one in the church having read the message from Paul could fail to be impressed with the work that Epaphroditus had done and with the high regard Paul felt for him.

Except for those few people who were quite contrary to the Christian gospel and causing trouble in the churches, Paul spoke positively about people and encouraged them in their faith. This is well illustrated in the following references, one to 'our sister Apphia', and another to Rufus' mother, 'who has always treated me like a son'.[13] Paul describes a large number of people in such terms as 'my dear friend Epaenetus', 'to Ampliatus, my dear friend in the fellowship of the Lord', and 'to my dear friend Persis who has done so much work for the Lord'.[14] Paul encouraged people to think well of themselves and have esteem for others. The effect of this was to make his helpers more effective in proclaiming the gospel.

Paul as agent of change

The first century AD was a period of great change within the Roman Empire and national, social and sexual distinctions as traditionally defined were being changed. Paul was an agent for change and is responsible for much of the impact of the Christian church on the Roman world by the end of the third century.

As he travelled throughout the Roman Empire he found that the social and cultural traditions of areas varied greatly and yet he saw how the Christian faith was applicable in each centre. Whenever local superstition or conventions clashed with the essence of the gospel he argued strongly against them, but on other matters which were purely cultural and customary, he carefully notes them and follows local tradition. Circumcision of Timothy and the avoidance of food offered to idols in Greece fall into these categories.

I believe that one of the reasons that the church in the twentieth century still has difficulties with some of Paul's teachings is that people do not understand the cultures and social customs of the various areas through which Paul travelled, established churches and to where he wrote his letters. The cultural differences in the role of women, for example, were vastly different in extremely conservative Jerusalem from what he found in, say, Antioch in Pisidia, Ephesus, Philippi, Athens or Rome. That is why Paul can be inconsistent on small details, such as whether a woman should speak in church as opposed to whether a woman should have her head covered when she does speak in church.

In particular there were three fundamental social attitudes which Paul helped change for all time: racism, the status of women, and the institution of slavery.

1. Racism
In the ancient world, ideas of racial superiority were not only acceptable but inevitable. Every community felt it was superior to every other community. The Jews were God's 'chosen people'. The Greeks regarded all others as 'barbarians'and the Romans regarded the rest of the world as 'inferior'. But Paul came preaching a doctrine which indicated that national superiority was a thing of the past. All mankind shared an inability to be right with God and a susceptibility to sin. No race was better than any other race and even those who felt themselves chosen of God still needed to be put right with God, 'because there is no difference at all: everyone has sinned and is far away from God's saving presence.'[15]

He tackled the difference between Jews and Gentiles boldly and declared:

You Gentiles by birth — called "the uncircumcised" by the Jews, who call themselves "the circumcised" (which refers to what men do to their bodies) — remember what you were in the past. At that time you were apart from Christ. But now, in union with Christ Jesus you, who used to be far away, have been brought near by the sacrificial death of Christ. For Christ himself has brought us peace by making Jews and Gentiles one people. With his own body he broke down the wall that separated them and kept them enemies. He abolished the Jewish law with its commandments and rules, in order to create out of the two races one new people in union with himself, in this way making peace. By his death on the cross Christ destroyed their enmity; by means of the cross he united both races into one body and brought them back to God.[16]

Paul was preaching a new nationhood — one people under God. That basic philosophy eroded national distinctions and has been the major reason why nations have changed in their attitudes towards racial superiority, and why it is regarded as heresy today for any people calling themselves Christian to hold a doctrine of racial superiority. That is why the Dutch Reformed Church of South Africa, which supported the Government's 'apartheid' policy, was classed by its sister churches of the World Alliance of Reformed Churches as committing heresy.

2. Women

A second cultural conflict is the vexed position of women in the church. The basic principle that Paul first enunciated is in the Galatian letter:

. . . so there is no difference between Jews and Gentiles, between slaves and free men, between men and women; you are all one in union with Christ Jesus.[17]

Paul indicates that those divisions have no place in the thought and practice of those who are united in Christ Jesus.

There are a number of instances where local circumstances seem to have overruled this principle. For example, in the letters to the church at Corinth we have some considerable confusion over the role of women in the church. It was a church in which there were disputes and Paul was called upon in some letter unknown to us today to arbitrate. It would be wrong to take the principle which he has enunciated and then deny it because of some pragmatic decisions he evidently must make.

The Wailing Wall: Jerusalem

The first of these decisions concerned covering the head during worship. I am sure that Paul wished he didn't have to arbitrate on such matters of dispute, but anyone who has worked in a church for any period of time knows how these matters of dispute over cultural and personal differences can become profoundly significant. In the church at Corinth the dispute was about whether or not men should have long hair and women should have short hair.

Furthermore in public worship it was believed that the heads of Christian men should be uncovered but those of Christian women should be covered. The interesting point is that in answering their problem Paul indicates that both men and women had a part in praying and proclaiming God's message in public. Both praying and prophesying were the most significant acts of leadership in church life and at Corinth women were involved in both roles.[18]

Paul indicated that they should judge for themselves 'whether it is proper for a woman to pray to God in public worship with nothing on her head. Why, nature itself teaches you that long hair on a man is a disgrace, but on a woman it is a thing of beauty. Her long hair has been given her to serve as a covering. But if anyone wants to argue about it, all I have to say is that neither we nor the churches of God have any other custom in worship.'[19] In the end the decision about head covering was left to individual judgment and as a matter of custom within the churches. I get the feeling that Paul is rather impatient of this whole argument and breaks off to speak about the significance of the Lord's Supper. Paul has stressed the keeping of an appropriate custom because in this cosmopolitan city, the new freedom found by Christian women was bringing some disrepute to the church.

However, we then come upon a significant difference later in the epistle when, in talking about orderly worship, Paul makes the point that married women are forbidden to speak in worship and are instead told to ask questions concerning faith of their husbands when they go home. If this is a rule, what about single women, unmarried, widowed, separated or divorced women, or women whose husbands were not Christians and who would never be able to explain Christian truth to them, or Christian women who were married to non-believers? The scriptures are silent upon what they should be doing in church. It also raises this point: How do you line up the two statements between those who preach and pray in public having their head covered and those who are forbidden to speak in public but who are to ask their husbands when they go home?

There are no clear answers.

It seems to me that Paul was replying to certain problems and as such gave pragmatic answers to specific local issues. He is not giving, in either case, basic principles for all time and all countries. In handling three issues in the local church's worship which were leading to noise and disruption (all speaking together in tongues, prophesying and asking their husbands questions), Paul gives pragmatic answers which ought not to become the basis for decisions on such matters as: can women be ordained as priests? The scriptural statements are irrelevant to that question!

Further insight is found if an examination is made of the women Paul encouraged into leadership in the local churches. At Philippi, Euodia and Syntyche who were leaders of the church had risen to a position of prominence, and then had a strong running disagreement. Paul did not instruct them to refrain from leadership but to learn to agree together.[20] In Corinth Paul came upon Priscilla and her husband Aquila. Both were Jewish Christians and together instructed the gifted Apollos of Alexandria where he was wrong and set up their home as a house church both in Ephesus and in Rome.

In the church at Rome, judging from Romans 16, there was a number of significant women in positions of leadership. Phoebe was described by Paul as 'a minister' even though other translations in recent centuries have rendered her job description as 'a servant', 'deaconess', 'one who holds office'. While it cannot be definitely stated that Phoebe was a minister, Paul used the same word to speak of himself as a minister of the gospel, of Apollos as minister, and of Stephanas.[21] The word as used in other locations of scripture definitely means 'minister' rather than 'deacon' or 'deaconess'. She must have had some position of ecclesiastical standing or authority because he asked his readers to receive her 'as God's people should, and give her any help she may need from you.'[22] This ministry role occupied by Phoebe is not accurately defined and is not to be necessarily equated with twentieth-century ministry concepts.

In the same chapter Paul makes mention of Andronicus and Junia who was, possibly, his wife, whom he described as 'fellow Jews who were in prison with me; they are well-known among the apostles, and they became Christians before I did.'[23] If Junia is his wife, then the question of women ministers suddenly shrinks in significance as here would be a woman apostle! One of the greatest preachers of the early church, John Chrysostom, believed Junia to be an apostle and praised God for such a female.

There are many women mentioned by name in the church of Rome to whom Paul sends greetings. At least twelve of them had some prominence, and nowhere is there any indication that the women named above

were debarred by Paul from praying or preaching in public worship. Over twenty women, named by Paul, fulfilled some role of leadership in the church, mostly in the western churches where society allowed women to play a greater role.

It is one of the strange facts of history that Paul is now looked upon as being restrictive about the role and rights of women within the early church, when he was in fact demonstrating a revolutionary change in the status of women.

Paul's principle of equality seems to have been limited in places where that principle was not accepted, but in areas where the church had social and cultural liberty, the principle of equality in leadership seems to have been exercised.

3. Slavery

A third issue was over slavery. Slavery was a basic, accepted way of life within the Roman Empire. Some people have condemned Paul for not initiating a radical move within society to outlaw slavery. It is true that Paul was no emancipist and that if he had roundly condemned slavery, then this wicked, dehumanising institution would have been outlawed from earth by Christians centuries earlier. That is, of course, if such an action by him had not totally destabilised the Roman Empire and led to the church being persecuted as politically undesirable.

What Paul did was to seek an even greater fundamental change: he dignified manual labour and proclaimed a brotherhood of believers.

As with matters of women in society, Paul seemed to act out of concern for the future of the church and stressed that Christians should obey the dictates of the government on such matters. However, by a new acceptance and treatment, they should build a new society in which race, sex and economic circumstances would not be determining factors.

It was the following teaching of Paul's on slaves when writing to Philemon about Onesimus that ultimately led to other Christians undermining the system of slavery in the world:

. . . and now he is not just a slave, but much more than a slave: he is a dear brother in Christ. How much he means to me! And how much more he will mean to you, both as a slave and as a brother in the Lord. [24]

Paul as a change agent was a quiet revolutionary. He never implied that God was wiping out the differences that exist between men and women, Jews and Gentiles, Romans and Greeks, slaves and free people, but Paul did something even deeper: he indicated that these differences no longer mattered in the kingdom of God and that they in no way affected a person's relationship with God through faith in Christ. Paul is interested in a new society where race, class, sex, social and economic standing do not matter.

Paul's teaching was too radical for the church. It found it difficult to take this teaching 'straight'. Consequently on all these matters there has been a watering down of Paul's position over the years and concessions to customs have been made.

For personal reading

Theme: A life fulfilled

MONDAY	Proclaiming Christ *Romans 15:14-21*
TUESDAY	Turning the world to Christ *Acts 17:1-9*
WEDNESDAY	In the power and Spirit of God *1 Corinthians 2:1-13*
THURSDAY	Christ's humility and greatness *Philippians 2:5-11*
FRIDAY	Life worthy of the Lord *Colossians 1:3-14*
SATURDAY	In praise of goodness and blessings *Philippians 4:8-13*
SUNDAY	Fight the good fight *1 Timothy 6:1-16*

For group study

Topic: Proclaiming the truth

1 Would·you agree with the author that people are expected to stand up for their faith? How can one do so effectively today?

2 What can we learn from the different styles of Paul's speeches?

3 Paul wrote letters out of personal concern for problem people. How involved are we willing to be with people who have problems? What are ways in which we can become more involved?

4 Make out a list of the letters of Paul. What are the main themes and how does each theme relate to our situation today?

5 Paul was a great encourager. Do you know of someone who always encourages others? What is your attitude towards other people?

6 In what ways do you see Paul as a radical agent of change? Was he successful?

10

Paul the Prophet

The film, 'Guess Who's Coming to Dinner?' is a delightful story of a liberal, outgoing, well-meaning family whose daughter is returning from overseas. They are overjoyed with the news that she is bringing her fiance home and are very impressed that she has chosen a doctor, a socially acceptable occupation among their liberal set. They open the door and see him: there is one thing she has forgotten to tell them — he is black! All of a sudden their liberal and open-minded attitudes come under challenge. How will they cope with their daughter in a racially mixed marriage? Because his parents have also been invited to the home that night a similar scene is enacted, for they do not know their son is marrying into a white family. The story revolves around how each of them resolves the situation . . .

Guess who is coming to dinner? At the end of time the Bible declares there will be a bridal feast of the Lamb of God[1] when everyone who loves God is invited. And guess who's coming? There will be some people there that we do not expect, and there will be some people there who do not expect us. The whole story of what is going to happen at the end of time and how that knowledge is revealed to us is part of what we call prophecy.

Paul fulfilled the role of a prophet as well as the other roles we have studied. Prophets were of profound significance right through the Bible. The role of the prophets began with Moses. The best-known prophets of the Old Testament were Amos, Hosea, Isaiah, Micah, Jeremiah, Ezekiel and Elijah. The arrangement of some of the Old Testament books is according to the prophets, with the former prophets being grouped together in the books of Joshua, Judges, Samuel and Kings; the latter prophets grouped together in Isaiah, Jeremiah and Ezekiel; and the minor prophets grouped at the close of the Old Testament, some twelve of them from Hosea to Malachi.

In the New Testament John the Baptist was regarded as a true prophet of God and Jesus was called a prophet. The church at Antioch had prophets and teachers among its leaders. The office and work of a prophet died out some time after the close of the third century of the Christian church.

The primary task of a prophet, judging from the original meaning of the word, was to announce news from God. The prophet announced God's word to his generation, reminded the people of Israel's election and covenant promise, rebuked them for sin and rebellion, and proclaimed the coming judgment and redemption of the people. There was, therefore, always an element of telling what was going to happen in the future, as well as proclaiming what the Lord wanted done then and there.

Consequently the prophet had a role both as a foreteller of things to come and a forthteller of God's word to his own generation.

Forthteller

Although the prophets of the Old Testament covered more than a thousand years of history, lived under the domination of a number of different conquerors and related in different ways to judges, kings and the priestly cult, there were some common themes found in their proclamation. Paul in his teaching fulfilled the most common elements found in the great Old Testament prophets.

Like many of them, Paul was an itinerant person, proclaiming from place to place the word of the Lord, and warning people to change and to seek the redemption that God offered. Like each of the great prophets Paul had experienced a call from God and was sent by him to proclaim his word.[2] Like Amos, Isaiah, Jeremiah and Ezekiel, Paul had been called and commissioned by God to proclaim his word. He felt obliged to do this, even though he might suffer persecution and difficulty, be ridiculed and scorned. Like these famous Old Testament prophets, he believed that he was bound up in the destiny of his people and that his personal suffering, rejection and even death were only part of his participation in the community's

response and rejection of God's word.

Four of the Old Testament prophets' great themes, also shared by John the Baptist and Jesus, were consistently found in the teachings of Paul:

1. Israel's place in history

The prophets were always proclaiming that God had chosen his people and that he would fulfil the promises of the covenant made with Abraham that they would become a great nation, and be a universal blessing. Paul proclaimed these truths in his addresses in the Jewish synagogues and his teaching to Jews when he addressed the synagogue in Antioch in Pisidia, and when he defended himself in Jerusalem. It seems that this was a pattern of Paul's preaching in Jewish circles.

2. The warning to turn from sin and rebellion against God

Paul, like the prophet of old, would call people to repentance, to turn from sin and rebellion against God, and to live a life in conformity with the moral precepts of the law. It seemed that this was a natural conclusion to his preaching, for he would proclaim even among the Greek philosophers in Athens, that 'God has overlooked the times when people did not know him, but now he commands all of them everywhere to turn away from their evil ways.'[3]

Like them, Paul believed that those outside the chosen race had also rebelled against God and needed to return to him. Israel's rebellion in sinfulness was shared by the whole of mankind. Paul made it clear when he wrote to the Romans that this rebellion could not go unpunished by God and that mankind's guilt would be dealt with by God's judgment.[4]

3. The compassion and redemption of God
Yet the prophet not only told of God's judgment against his people, but promised the compassion and redemption of God. He showed mercy, kindness and grace in dealing with his wayward people. Paul likewise expressed God's forgiveness. His call was for people to return to him and to receive the mercy of God. Words like *grace, mercy* and *love* became the great theme words in his preaching.

4. The call to repentance and acceptance of redemption
The prophets always completed their major addresses with God's call to the people to turn back to him in repentance and to receive from him the promise of a new future, of being at one with God. His word would accomplish that, and through them all the nations of the world would be blessed. It would be through the suffering Messiah that this blessing would come.

This message of the prophet was the heart of Paul's gospel of redemption. In continuing these major themes, Paul was standing in the traditions of the great men of God who spoke out his message with both warning and compassion.

Foreteller

The future was central to Paul's message. The end of time and the great climax of God's purposes gave point and purpose to life for the Christian. We are to live with God making us 'holy in every way'[5] and keeping our whole being — spirit, soul and body — free from every fault at the coming of our Lord Jesus Christ. His apocalyptic message gave to the believers hope, comfort, encouragement and purpose in their suffering. Paul stressed that the believers not only dwelt here in the present but were already part of that future life:

Actually everything belongs to you: this world, life and death, the present and the future — all these are yours, and you belong to Christ, and Christ belongs to God. [6]

While the believer lives in the flesh, the believer also lives in the spirit. Heaven is here and now, not only in the age to come.

Paul's teaching about the future, like many other aspects of his teaching, grew out of a pastoral problem. Paul had founded the church in Thessalonica and taught them about the coming of Jesus. He had to leave the Christians there to go on with his missionary journey throughout Greece. After he had left, some of the members of the church had died and consequently this raised a number of questions in their minds. They contacted Paul about these questions: What about the people who died believing in Jesus but who did not see his return? What about others of them who were still alive — would they see the Lord's return in their lifetime? When would the Lord return?

Paul's answer was one of the reasons for writing his first letter to the Christians at Thessalonica:

What we are teaching you now is the Lord's teaching: we who are alive on the day the Lord comes will not go ahead of those who have died. There will be a shout of command, the archangel's voice, the sound of God's trumpet and the Lord himself will come down from heaven. Those who have died believing in Christ will rise to life first; then we who are living at that time will be gathered up along with them in the clouds to meet the Lord in the air. And so we will always be with the Lord.[7]

1. The age to come

The church is vital to the age to come, not as a vehicle of proclaiming the truth, or as a means of propaganda about the faith only, but as the already existing first-fruits of that age. Paul said 'We have the Spirit as the first of God's gifts . . . as we wait for God to make us his sons and set our whole being free.'[8] The gift of the Holy Spirit is the guarantee of more yet to come. The whole of creation will be transformed and in fact that future age has already broken into this era of historical time. This age has about it the death throes and is already rattling into extinction. The believer not only knows that the Lord will come in the future but can sense his presence now.

2. The second coming of the Lord

In almost every letter in the New Testament there is reference to the second coming of Jesus. There are eighteen major references to the

second coming and seven out of each ten chapters of the New Testament have a reference to the return of Christ.

Jesus himself promised that he would come again.[9] The early apostles proclaimed Jesus' return as central to their gospel, and Peter and John held to the truth as providing meaning for the way Christians must live in difficult times. Paul likewise stressed the great significance of the second coming of Jesus. The early Christians greeted each other with 'Maranatha — Our Lord, come!'[10]

Paul taught that Jesus will come in power and glory from heaven surrounded by his angels, and with the Christians who had died before his coming. When the Lord returns he will judge both the living and the dead, and receive to himself those who are faithful. Paul told the Christians at Corinth that the dead will rise with a new eternal body and those who have survived will be transformed:

We shall all be changed in an instant, as quickly as the blinking of an eye. For when the trumpet sounds, the dead will be raised, never to die again, and we shall all be changed. For what is mortal must be changed into what is immortal; what will die must be changed into what cannot die. So when this takes place, and the mortal has been changed into the immortal, then the scripture will come true: 'Death is destroyed; Victory is complete!'[11]

The believers will be gathered together with him from all the known world. At this time 'in honour of the name of Jesus all beings in heaven, on earth, and in the world below will fall on their knees, and all will openly proclaim that Jesus Christ is Lord, to the glory of God the Father.'[12]

Then the judgment will occur: 'Final judgment must wait until the Lord comes; he will bring to light the dark secrets and expose the hidden purposes of people's minds. And then everyone will receive from God the praise he deserves.'[13] Those who have believed in Jesus need fear no condemnation for they have been put right with God through faith and consequently do not come under condemnation. But those who have refused the gospel will be destroyed and their judgment is to be excluded from God eternally. The believers will enter into God's presence.

Paul thus preached the second coming of the Lord with great vigour, encouraging the believers to look forward to their future with him.

3. The omega point

But Christ was to do more than just take the believers to himself and separate the non-believers from God's presence. Christ is a cosmic Christ who was the agent of God in creation, and he will be the omega point to which all history is moving. 'Through the Son, then, God decided to bring the whole universe back to himself. God made peace through his Son's sacrificial death on the cross and so brought back to himself all things, both on earth and in heaven.'[14] The whole of creation is looking forward to a time of renewal and at the second coming Jesus will usher in the new age that will see the renewal of heaven and earth. Until that time creation is in travail.

Because we believe in him, we now have a promise that we will become as he is. There is a spiritual perfection that is promised to us. This can be appropriated now and Christians can keep growing to be more like him. Every believer now becomes a new person in Christ and we are being changed into his glory.

Paul taught that when the Son hands over the kingdom to the Father there will be a re-creation of the whole universe, a new heaven and a new earth. God will rule over all. This world will be free from all corruption.

4. The resurrection factor

The key to all of this lies in the resurrection of Jesus. Because of his resurrection from the dead we too will share in his resurrection with life and immortality. As a pharisee Paul had believed in the resurrection of the body which was one of the distinguishing features between Pharisees and Sadducees.

But it was Paul's actual meeting with the resurrected Jesus that changed a belief into a passion. Paul now understood the resurrection of the body in a new way. He replied to those who did not believe in the resurrection of the body with a new concept of resurrection: not a Greek philosophical concept of the immortality of the soul, nor a bodily assumption of people into heaven; instead, a transformation of a mortal body into an immortal one. Just as the seed dies upon being buried in the ground to give birth to new life, so our faith enables us to be changed from a mortal to an immortal body:

'For we know that when
this tent we live in —
our body here on earth
— is torn down, God will
have a house in heaven
for us to live in, a home
he himself has made,
which will last for ever.
While we live in this
earthly tent, we groan
with a feeling of
oppression; it is not that
we want to get rid of
our earthly body, but
that we want to have
the heavenly one put on
over us, so that what is
mortal will be
transformed by life.'[15]

As Christ was raised from the dead, so the believers who died believing in him will be raised with a new spiritual body and we will be made like his glorious body, able to abide with him and the Father for ever. Because God raised Christ from the dead, our resurrection is not just a hope but an assurance of what will happen.

5. The sacraments

It is in this forward-looking, prophetic vein that Paul speaks about the sacraments. Baptism and the Lord's Supper are not just rituals of the church for initiation and remembrance, but they are in themselves prophetic, pointing to our new life and presence with the Lord. Paul was the first to write about both.

The key to our understanding of baptism lies in our identification with the death, burial and resurrection of Jesus. He taught that when we were baptised, we were baptised into his death, into his resurrection, into his body, and into new life. The very form of baptism by immersion symbolises our old life being buried beneath the water and being raised to a new life. Paul would not equate baptism as a new form of circumcision to initiate babies into the kingdom. Neither would he declare that Christians were to be saved from immorality, sin and moral imperfection by baptism.

Paul left the administration of baptism to other ministers who travelled with him, to avoid people becoming proud of the fact that they had been baptised by him personally and therefore setting up a party under his own name. He anticipated that every believer would be baptised. There is no direct evidence in the New Testament for the baptism of infants. Through our baptism we appropriate what Christ has done for us and our baptism is a pledge of God's blessings both now and in the future.

The Lord's Supper is referred to by Paul only in his first letter to the Corinthians. His instructions about what happened on the night Jesus was betrayed were conveyed to him personally by the Lord. While Paul speaks of the communion of the Lord's Supper as a memorial, as fellowship and communion of Christians and as a participation in his blessing, it is also a prophetic sacrament in that 'every time you eat this bread and drink from this cup you proclaim the Lord's death until he comes.'[16] Paul also mentions that the Lord's Supper, if partaken of unworthily, is a judgment upon the participant and he indicated that some had become ill and even died, bringing judgment on themselves, because of the careless way in which they had treated the Lord's Supper.

While these paragraphs are not detailed teaching on the significance of both baptism and the Lord's Supper, they are an aspect of Paul's prophetic ministry, for both baptism and the Lord's Supper point to our life not only here in fellowship with Christ, but in the age to come.

Paul stood within the traditions of the great prophets of the Old and New Testaments in his proclamation, not only of how Christians should believe and behave, but how we should look to the future with hope and expectation.

For personal reading

Theme: Jesus is coming again

MONDAY	Caught up with the Lord *1 Thessalonians 4:13-18*
TUESDAY	Raised in glory *1 Corinthians 15:42-58*
WEDNESDAY	Conquerors through Christ *Romans 8:28-39*
THURSDAY	The Lord comes to judge *1 Corinthians 4:1-5*
FRIDAY	Chosen for salvation *2 Thessalonians 2:1-16*
SATURDAY	In remembrance of me *1 Corinthians 11:19-33*
SUNDAY	Baptised in Christ *Romans 6:1-11*

For group study

Topic: Our Lord comes!

1 What do you understand by the word 'prophet'?

2 What is the role and function of a prophet?

3 How do we know that Jesus will come again?

4 In what ways is the resurrection of Jesus important? Where does it fit with the second coming of Jesus?

5 What does the Bible say about the prophetic character of the sacraments of baptism and the Lord's Supper?

11

Paul the Prisoner

Any picture of Paul taken during his life would have had to be a moving picture. He was never still long enough for any other kind. If the twentieth century were to follow Paul's itinerary we would do so by having a team from '60 Minutes' follow him on his intrepid journeys, interviewing him in difficult situations and flying news teams to remote places in order to grab a news story from the midst of a riot or a stoning. He would be commissioned by some university to take a sabbatical year's leave, to write a book and to deliver in print his theology and thoughts.

Although the first century had none of these techniques, the result was almost the same: Luke despatched himself to travel with Paul and wrote first-hand eyewitness accounts of many of the events of his journeys, his account being called *The Acts of the Apostles*. Paul never took a sabbatical year or wrote a book. Instead, by the force of circumstances while imprisoned, he wrote letters to those churches he could not now personally visit. Those epistles from prison make up the bulk of our New Testament.

In this sense we can be thankful for the times of imprisonment faced by Paul, because it was only enforced imprisonment which caused him to write instead of lecturing and speaking.

Imprisonment was not used as a punishment for people as such in New Testament times: accused persons were being held in custody until judgment. People who were regarded as dangerous, who were arrested for crimes, and who were taken into temporary custody, were imprisoned in what were some of the worst detention centres imaginable. Sometimes these consisted of dungeons, deep wells, unsanitary cells and sometimes 'the court of the guard' which was detention within the guards' quarters.

Punishment for the accused in the first century was by crucifixion (for only the worst offenders), beheading, impaling and stoning as capital punishment; being condemned to the mines for the term of one's natural life (*damnatus in metallum*); scourging; hauling a millstone or a grindstone on an endless track; or by branding with a red hot iron on the forehead 'F' for *fugitivus* in the case of a runaway slave. Exile into a lonely place, such as John's Isle of Patmos, was frequent for political prisoners. People who were imprisoned until their trials were usually held by chains, fetters and stocks.

However, it was illegal to treat a Roman citizen by these means of punishment. Augustus' decree *lex Julia de vi publica* had made it a crime to imprison or scourge a Roman citizen. Because of his citizenship Paul had such immunity. Occasionally he called upon that immunity, on one occasion saying to the police officers:

We were not found guilty of any crime, yet [the Roman officials] whipped us in public — and we are Roman citizens! Then they threw us in prison. And now they want to send us away secretly. Not at all! The Roman officials themselves must come here and let us out.' The police officers reported these words to the Roman officials; and when they heard that Paul and Silas were Roman citizens, they were afraid. So they went and apologised to them; then they let them out of the prison and asked them to leave the city.[1]

However, there were times when this immunity was not respected:

Five times I was given the thirty-nine lashes by the Jews; three times I was whipped by the Romans; and once I was stoned.[2]

A Roman citizen could be tried by the local governor in council or by direct appeal to the Emperor himself. Paul was to use both of these rights at times when it was obvious he could not receive a fair trial from those prejudiced against him.

Paul had a favourite saying which he dictated to a number of churches: 'We have complete victory!' It is important to note where Paul was declaring complete victory: it was while he was in stocks in a prison somewhere! On most of these occasions he had suffered excruciating pain through physical punishment and was confined awaiting further judgment. Yet in such circumstances he declared complete victory for the faith through what had happened to him. An autobiography of the apostle could have been written simply round the prisons in which he spent time under the heading 'Prisons I have known'!

However, there is very little evidence of the circumstances of those prisons even though Paul wrote out of them. He was not full of complaints and rarely alluded to his circumstances except for occasional comments about being in bonds. On one occasion in his final letter from Rome to Timothy, he spoke of his personal needs:

Do your best to come to me soon. Demas . . . has deserted me . . . Crescens went to Galatia, and Titus to Dalmatia. Only Luke is with me. Get Mark and bring him with you,

because he can help me in the work.
I sent Tychicus to Ephesus. When
you come, bring my coat that I left
in Troas with Carpus; bring the
books too, especially the ones made
of parchment.[3]

Archeologists have been able to
recover some sites where Paul
may have been imprisoned, but
because prisons were usually deep
dark recesses within otherwise
nondescript buildings, the
likelihood of finding the cells in
which Paul was held is most
remote.

Imprisoned in Philippi

Paul and Silas were arrested for
healing a demented girl. The
owners of the slave girl saw that
their opportunity to earn money,
by using her mentally unbalanced
ravings to predict fortunes for
people, was gone. In anger they
had Paul and Silas charged and
imprisoned for loss of income. It
is interesting that Timothy and
Luke were not gaoled even though
they were present with Paul and
Silas. This is probably because
they were Gentiles and not
Jewish-looking. This event
occurred during a wave of anti-
semitism which spread through

the empire after the expulsion of
Jews from Rome by the Emperor
Claudius in AD 49. It was in the
following months that Paul was in
Philippi. Both Paul and Silas were
beaten by the Lictors' rods, and
cast into prison with their feet in
stocks and chained to the wall. It
was at midnight while they were
singing hymns that they were
miraculously released through an
earthquake which separated their
stocks, and they were able to
walk out through the fallen doors.
The gaoler rushed in with a light
and, supposing the prisoners had
escaped, was about to kill himself
rather than face the disgrace. Paul
and Silas spoke of their faith to
him with the result that he
washed them, bound up their
wounds, believed in Jesus Christ
and was baptised. The following
morning the Roman authorities
ordered the police officers to
release the men and Paul, as a
Roman citizen, demanded an
apology from the public officials
for being whipped. The speed
with which the apology arrived
indicates how well they knew the
law that placed them under threat
of death for imprisoning and
whipping Roman citizens.

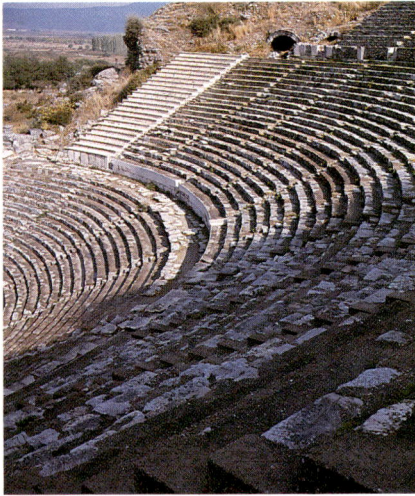

Theatre at Ephesus: Turkey

Imprisoned in Ephesus

We wish we had more details of this imprisonment. Paul indicated that 'I have, as it were, fought wild beasts here in Ephesus'[4] and that 'there is a real opportunity [in Ephesus] for a great and worthwhile work, even though there are many opponents.'[5] He also wrote:

We want to remind you, brothers, of the trouble we had in the province of Asia [a way of referring to the area around Ephesus]. The burdens laid upon us were so great and so heavy that we gave up all hope of staying alive. We felt that the death sentence had been passed on us. But this happened so that we should rely, not on ourselves, but only on God, who raises the dead. From such terrible dangers of death he saved us.[6]

We know that in Ephesus he was strongly opposed by the local silversmiths under the leadership of Demetrius and the Jews from the local synagogue who plotted against him. These Jews may have been ones who 'saw Paul in the temple. They stirred up the whole crowd and grabbed Paul.'[7] The riot continued and the crowd gathered in the theatre. This beautiful theatre in Ephesus still stands today and seated 24,500 people. As a result Gaius and Aristarchus, two Macedonians who were travelling with Paul, were dragged off for punishment.

It is possible that Paul was imprisoned at this time and, if so, he probably wrote some of his letters from this prison, particularly the letters to the Philippians and to Philemon. It is possible that it was here Paul met Onesimus the runaway slave from Colossae, just one hundred miles to the east. However, Onesimus could just as easily have met Paul in Rome because, especially in those days, 'all roads lead to Rome'. A tower overlooking the city called St Paul's prison is quite unlikely to have been the site of Paul's imprisonment, yet it does keep alive the tradition that Paul was imprisoned during his time in Ephesus.

Main street at Ephesus

Imprisoned in Jerusalem

Paul realised that returning to Jerusalem after the third missionary journey would be dangerous. While he was on his way toward Jerusalem Agabus came from Jerusalem and warned him against continuing. Paul made a significant financial collection from among the Christian Gentiles to help the poor, the widows and the orphans of Jerusalem. He also paid the expenses of four Hebrew Christians who were involved in a Nazarite rite, and he fasted. He believed this would pacify the opponents of the early church. However, the Jews from Turkey, probably from Ephesus, thought he had taken Trophimus from Ephesus, whom they recognised, into the sacred precincts of the temple, an area out-of-bounds to Gentiles, a fact affirmed by two inscriptions discovered by archeologists in 1871 and in 1931. In three languages it stated: 'No foreigner may enter within the barricade which surrounds the Temple and its enclosure. Anyone who is caught doing so will have

himself to blame for his ensuing death.' In the riot that followed Paul had to be rescued by soldiers stationed in the Castle of Antonia.

Paul was imprisoned overnight in the Tower of Antonia, one of the four towers erected by Herod the Great. It was while he was in this prison that his sister's son came and warned Claudius Lysias that there was a threat against Paul's life. Claudius was not willing for further disturbances to take place in the heart of the city so, in the middle of the night, he ordered 200 soldiers, seventy horsemen and 200 spearmen to take Paul and to march to safety in Caesarea. Paul was provided with a horse for the journey and the soldiers were force-marched during the night to Antipatris, thirty-five miles distant. There the foot soldiers were left behind and the next day Paul, still under guard and accompanied by seventy cavalry, rode on a further twenty-five miles to Caesarea on the coast, taking with him a letter of explanation to Governor Felix. Here Paul was kept once more in prison under guard in the governor's headquarters.

Imprisoned in Caesarea

When Paul arrived at Caesarea with the detachment of horsemen keeping him safe, he was taken immediately to the governor's fort and kept under guard in the *praetorium*. This prison was going to be Paul's home for the next two years. The guard room in the old palace was apparently of some size and it was possible for Christians in Caesarea to visit him during that time.

Herod the Great built this

magnificent city on the shores of the Mediterranean Sea as a tribute to Caesar and as a place for rest and recreation for himself and for Roman troops stationed in Palestine. The Roman centurion whom Peter converted was stationed here and a church began here following his conversion. It was here that Paul was tried before Festus and Herod Agrippa before he sailed to Rome.

Paul made a very precise defence before the high priest Ananias, some elders and a lawyer named Tertullus who appeared with the charges against Paul before the governor Felix. Paul's defence before Felix is a masterpiece of presentation. Paul discussed goodness, self-control and the coming day of judgment with the result that Felix was afraid. The governor was living in an adulterous relationship at the time and Paul's blunt words must have hurt him. Marcus Antonius Felix was a remarkable man, a freedman who rose with administrative ability and skill to be governor of Judea. Tacitus said, 'he exercised the power of a king with the mind of a slave.'[8]

He hoped that Paul would eventually buy his freedom from him and frequently spoke to Paul with an eye for some personal return. After being in prison for two years, 'Porcius Festus succeeded Felix as governor. Felix wanted to gain favour with the Jews so he left Paul in prison.'[9] So once more Paul had to defend himself, this time before the new governor Festus. After hearing Paul's defence he still left him in prison until the visit to Caesarea of King Agrippa and his sister Bernice. Once more Paul gave testimony to his faith in Christ and, before the king, the governor and the military chiefs, Paul defended himself telling of his conversion and his preaching.

At the end of this presentation the decision was made: 'This man has not done anything for which he should die or be put in prison'[10] but because Paul had appealed to the Emperor it was decided that he should be then sent to Rome. Paul insisted on his case being heard before the Emperor because the Jews kept insisting that they should try Paul under their own jurisdiction and Paul knew that there could be only one result if they were in charge. Paul was to face at least four more years of imprisonment before going to Rome.

During his time in Caesarea the local Christians provided him with support, visiting him and giving him encouragement. In Caesarea were Philip and his four daughters, Cornelius and all his household who had been converted by the apostle Peter, and some like Agabus who would have travelled out from Jerusalem.

Caesarea

Caesarea

Imprisoned in Rome

'And so we came to Rome.'[11] This was the destination for which Paul had longed. After landing at Puteoli and staying there seven days with local Christians, Paul moved up the Via Appia, so called because the road commenced under the 550-year-old aqueduct built by Appius which brought water into Rome. While they were still forty miles from Rome they were met by Christians who came out of the city to meet him at the place of the Three Taverns in the Appii Forum. When Paul was brought to Rome he was imprisoned under the care of the personal guard of a *stratopedarchos* or camp commandant. For the next two years Paul stayed under house arrest, living in his own house at his own expense, but nevertheless still chained to a soldier. This soldier was changed every eight hours and so in each twenty-four hour period Paul had at least three persons as a captive congregation. Some of these soldiers eventually became Christians and amongst them 'those who belong to the Emperor's household.'[12] While he was in this house Jews came to visit him and to ask him to explain more about his understanding of the Messiah. A number of Christians constantly visited and stayed with him. Rome was the home of Priscilla and Aquila and others had become Christians dating back even to the first day of Pentecost. By the time Paul wrote the letter to the church at Rome, as is evidenced from the sixteenth chapter, there were scores of people who were believers in the Roman capital under the leadership of people like Phoebe. Some of their names indicate that they belonged to noble families. Some years earlier Peter had visited the church at Rome and the church had grown from his ministry.

It was while Paul was in this Roman prison that he could say:

The things that have happened to me have really helped the progress of the gospel. As a result, the whole palace guard and all the others here know that I am in prison because I am a servant of Christ. And my being in prison has given most of the brothers more confidence in the Lord, so that they grow bolder all the time to preach the message fearlessly.[13]

It is probable that after some two years Paul was released following a successful first hearing. There is some evidence that in the year AD 62 the Emperor Nero, in an act of clemency, released numerous prisoners who had not been brought to trial because of lack of prosecution witnesses.

Paul now probably had a period of two years of freedom during which Rome was the base of his ministry. He had with him Mark, Jesus Justus, Aristarchus, Timothy and Luke as well as some others. It may have been here that he had the support of Epaphroditus. Paul not only helped to strengthen the church during these two years of comparative freedom in Rome, but tradition indicates he may have visited Spain, that far western country which had been one of his prime objectives.

There was plenty of opportunity for Paul to preach the gospel. Approximately one million people, half of whom were slaves, lived in the city of Rome in a densely-populated community only twelve miles in circumference. We read that it was expensive to live in the heart of the city, that rentals were extremely high, but that the gift brought by Epaphroditus from Philippi possibly helped Paul to pay his way. Paul probably stayed in one of Rome's large tenement buildings, some of which were so large they were called *insulae* — islands. Shops and offices filled the ground floor and people lived on at least seven storeys above. Roman writers like Juvenal commented about having to climb 200 steps to reach their top-storey flats.

With the burning of Rome in AD 64, Paul's freedom was quickly brought to an end. The five-day fire which started on 18 July burnt out a large section of the city.

In AD 62 Nero had married Poppaeia who was a Jewish proselyte. He had a love/hate relationship with her and because of her support for the Jews, she probably helped establish his hatred for them. The historians Tacitus and Suetonius both refer to the rumour that Nero himself may have ordered the fire in order to clear out a large part of Rome for rebuilding.

Tacitus says: 'Consequently, to get rid of the report Nero fastened the guilt and inflicted the most exquisite tortures on a class hated for its abominations, called Christians by the populace. Christus, from whom the name had its origin, suffered the extreme penalty during the reign of Tiberius at the hands of one of our procurators, Pontius Pilate,

and a most mischievous superstition, thus checked for the moment, again broke out not only in Judea, the first source of the evil, but even in Rome, where all things hideous and shameful from every part of the world find their centre and become popular. Accordingly, an arrest was first made of all who pleaded guilty; then, upon their information, an immense multitude was convicted, not so much of the crime of firing the city, as of hatred against mankind. Mockery of every sort was added to their deaths. Covered with the skins of beasts, they were torn by dogs and perished, or were nailed to crosses, or were doomed to the flames and burnt, to serve as a nightly illumination when daylight had expired. Nero offered his gardens for the spectacle, and was exhibiting a show in the circus, while he mingled with the people in the dress of a charioteer or stood aloft on a car. Hence, even for criminals who deserved extreme and exemplary punishment, there arose a feeling of compassion; for it was not, as it seemed, for the public good, but to glut one man's cruelty, that they were being destroyed.'[14]

It is probable that Paul died at this time. It must have been about then he said: 'The time is here for me to leave this life. I have done my best in the race, I have run the full distance, and I have kept the faith. And now there is waiting for me the prize of victory awarded for a righteous life, the prize which the Lord, the righteous Judge, will give me on that day — and not only to me, but to all who wait with love for him to appear.'[15]

St Paul's Outside the Walls: Rome

It is possible that Paul was imprisoned in the Mamertine prison. He was possibly executed by beheading with a sword. This could have been at Aquae Salviae, at the third milestone on the Ostian Way. The Christians erected a small monument on the site and a basilica was built over the traditional tomb of Paul. This church, *San Paolo fuori le mura* (St Paul's Outside the Walls), was completed in AD 398 and remained standing for 1400 years until fire destroyed it in 1823. The present church was built over it. In 1835 during the rebuilding, archeologists found a fourth-century tablet in the lowest part of the basilica's crypt with the words 'To Paul, Apostle and Martyr'. He had been buried in what the Romans regarded as a pagan burial ground. Paul would have regarded this as appropriate.

He was buried in the city that persecuted him, which itself was to fall to the faith that Paul proclaimed. The day would come when people throughout the world would call their dogs 'Nero' and their sons 'Paul'.

Looking back over his years of imprisonment and suffering for his faith, Paul could confidently say that he was victorious in spite of everything.

For personal reading

Theme: Bound in body but free in spirit

MONDAY	Believe and be saved *Acts 16:16-34*
TUESDAY	Jesus is the Christ *Colossians 2:1-15*
WEDNESDAY	Victory in Christ *1 Thessalonians 2:13-20*
THURSDAY	Assurance to witnesses *Acts 23:1-11*
FRIDAY	A prisoner in command Acts 27:21-38
SATURDAY	Preaching the Kingdom of God *Acts 28:16-30*
SUNDAY	Imprisonment for Christ *Philippians 1:12-18*

For group study

Topic: Complete victory for the faith

1 What was Paul's response to his beatings, imprisonments, stonings and persecutions? Why did he react in this way?

2 How should Christians today face persecutions? Can you share some modern examples?

3 Paul seemed to be gainfully active in spite of being imprisoned. What were some of the results of his work and witness in prisons?

4 Rome was special in Paul's life. What were some of the highlights of his visit to Rome?

5 How would you describe the life of Paul? What was the most significant thing in his life? What can we learn from him?

12

Paul the Person

Paul was born some time about 4 to 3 BC and died in AD 64-65. He was converted for Christ halfway through his life in about AD 32, hence he had 32 or 33 years of ministry. The life of Paul as we know it from the records covers a span of some sixteen years; the rest is silence. He did not keep a diary and was not interested in passing on details about his travels, most of the delights and difficulties he faced, or the statistical results of his missionary endeavours.

How unlike a contemporary evangelist or missionary!

Nothing is recorded of Paul's normal methods of ministry when he stayed in one place. For example, when he spent about three years in Ephesus, we know he spent three months preaching in the synagogues and two years lecturing in the hall of Tyrannus and that he made a visit to Corinth, but of his style of ministry in such a settled pastorate we know nothing at all.

However, when Luke was with Paul, there is more information. The 'we' passages written by Luke as a personal record in Acts cover a number of important places during his missionary journeys: from Troas to Philippi on the second tour; from Philippi to Miletus on the third missionary journey; from Miletus to Jerusalem; from Caesarea to Rome. These passages are vivid and trustworthy in their detail.

The speeches of Paul in the Acts of the Apostles were handed down to Luke by either Paul himself or by some others who were there and who kept a record of them. Luke seems to be present only at the speech at Miletus. The other speeches, probably a summary from Paul, seem to lack the emphasis that Paul would have made on the death of Christ upon the cross and its effects, and the coming judgment of God.

However, the epistles and the Acts of the Apostles provide us with enough evidence to indicate that Paul lived the complete life.

Paul's life 'in Christ'

Paul was not married during his Christian life, although an earlier marriage is possible. Some would claim that because he lacked both wife and children, of necessity he did not know what it was to live a complete life. Yet Paul made it very clear that his constant attention to the church was similar to a responsibility to a wife, and his care for young Timothy and Titus and others who became preachers of the gospel was like that of a father to a son.

Paul certainly lived as full a life as any of whom we have record.

While his personal appearance and specialist skills as an orator apparently caused some people to feel that he was in no way outstanding, and although he suffered throughout all of his life with a debilitating ailment or illness which limited him, Paul made the most of every opportunity he had and didn't allow personal weakness to hamper him. To follow any of the thousands of miles he walked through very rugged terrain is to capture a vision of the resoluteness and determination of will that constantly pushed him onward.

An example of this strength of purpose can be seen at the time when crowds of people attacked Paul in Lystra:

They stoned Paul and dragged him out of the town, thinking that he was dead. But when the believers gathered around him, he got up and went back into the town. The next day he and Barnabas went on to Derbe. Paul and Barnabas preached the good news in Derbe and won many disciples.[1]

Only a remarkable person could continue under those circumstances.

The key to Paul's strength of purpose was that his life was 'in Christ'. Although Paul used a number of terms to describe Jesus — Christ, Son of God, Lord, Messiah, Second Adam — it was 'in Christ' that was his favourite description of his relationship with the Lord. It was this oneness that he had with Christ that enabled him to endure so much.

Paul's training

Paul was a Jew by race and by religion, and was always proud of belonging to God's people. He was a 'Hebrew of the Hebrews', spoke Hebrew, and constantly spoke of the Law, of righteousness, of the promises made by God, and of the coming judgment.

Yet he was a Jew of the Diaspora, a Hellenist Jew, who was influenced by Greek culture. He wrote Greek, read the Old Testament in Greek, and felt at home in the Greek world of sophisticated philosophy and argument. His birthplace was at the centre of a large Greek university.

He was also a Roman citizen, the son of a Roman citizen, and he used the Roman law, the Roman roads and the Roman peace to take the gospel throughout the known world. He was at home relating to Roman soldiers, guards and governors, and was happy living and working in the cities, in courts and with the military.

But Paul was also Christian, and that meant that he was one of the new people of God who were not differentiated because of their race or sex or language or economic or social conditions.

Paul's achievements

God in his wisdom used Paul's rich and varied background to achieve his divine purposes.

His first achievement for God was *the taking of Christianity from the east to the west*. In doing this, he visited major cities one after the other and left behind established groups of believers often under the leadership of one of his young ministers who travelled with him. The influence of his ministry in the west, therefore, was permanent.

Paul became *the driving force of evangelism* in the early church. Although Peter helped spread the faith in taking the message to Caesarea and then later eventually to Rome, and others like Philip and his four daughters were quick to respond to the evangelistic ministry of the church, it was Paul more than any who carried out the great commission of Jesus to take the gospel into the known world. His example not only inspired other first century Christians to continue to proclaim the gospel to all men everywhere, but has ever since been the focal point in every renewal of evangelism.

Paul was *the first great theologian of the Christian church*. Although not a systematic theologian in the style of Thomas

Aquinas, John Calvin, or Karl Barth, Paul laid the foundation upon which all other theologians have worked. He emphasised that no one could save himself and his emphasis is needed in a secular world where men pride themselves on personal competence. Paul developed the concepts of *adoption* into the family of God which he had borrowed from the human family; the concept of our *emancipation* from the bondage of sin, which he took from slavery; the concept of *propitiation*, from the idea of sacrifice; and the concept of *reconciliation* from the idea of friendship. But Paul's great contribution to theological understanding was his emphasis upon *justification*, a theme he developed from the law courts. This became the keystone to Paul's theological understanding. No one is made righteous before God by his own efforts but we are justified by faith through God's grace. God in his mercy treats us as righteous, not imputing to us the guilt that is due to us, but instead treating us as acceptable and sinless because we are received before him in Christ. Only God's mercy and grace enables this.

In every generation since, whenever these theological terms of the apostle have been studied, there has been a fresh outburst of vitality within the church as people have understood the nature of salvation.

Paul *changed Christianity from a Jewish sect to a world movement*. Paul was a citizen of the world and he took the gospel into the secular cities of the empire and from there it became a world movement.

Paul's extensive influence

Paul's achievements have been due in part to the extent of his travels in proclaiming the gospel. First, in the seventeen silent years after his conversion he travelled throughout Syria, back to Damascus and Jerusalem to Caesarea and Cilicia. Congregations of the believers were established during these visits. Second, he travelled throughout Turkey and Cyprus on what is called the first missionary journey, establishing churches and revisiting those he had visited before. Third, he took the gospel message back through Turkey and into Europe, travelling through Macedonia and Greece once more establishing congregations of the faithful in what is called the second missionary journey. Fourth, his missionary journeys took him through the Aegean Sea and Greece visiting earlier established congregations and establishing new ones on his third missionary journey. Fifth, he took a long trip throughout Israel, Cyprus, Malta, Italy and on to Rome. In spite of the severe handicaps on this journey, the shipwreck and the problems of being always under guard, Paul continued to witness to his faith, establishing believers wherever he stayed. Sixth, his final visits are the unknown ones made between the years AD 61 and 65. Tradition has it that he visited Spain, Crete, Macedonia and Achaia.

Another reason for his achieving so much has been the quality of his writings. His epistles were sent where he could not go himself. Paul may have written many letters of which about a dozen survive. The reason they survive is that right from the time of reception they were regarded as special, as having the authority of the apostle to the Gentiles and being valuable for spiritual growth. They were possibly copied into a codex in Ephesus in the second century and circulated around all the churches. Certainly they were widely known by AD 150 and were already accepted as significant documents under the inspiration of God.

His influence on movements in the history of the church has been considerable. Many of the greatest of the church's theologians, evangelists and leaders have been converted and inspired through Paul's writings. St Augustine was converted through the reading of Romans 13. Thomas Aquinas wrote his great commentaries specialising in Paul's theology. Martin Luther was converted and brought to profound insight on the nature of our justification by faith while pondering Romans 1. John Wesley was converted on 24 May, 1738, in Aldersgate Street, London, while reading Luther's preface to his commentary on Paul's epistle to the Romans. Immediately after World War I Karl Barth, one of the most potent theological forces of the twentieth century, published his commentary on the Epistle to the Romans.

Whenever Paul has been rediscovered and his writings read afresh there has been a new outbreak of evangelism and witness to the faith in Christ.

Paul's constant themes

It is believed that where men
and women of faith make the
same emphases today as Paul did,
God still blesses them with
growth in their personal lives and
in their witness to Christ.

(a) The grace of God

Paul knew that he had sinned
greatly, had resisted God's grace
and opposed the Lord Jesus
Christ. 'But God was merciful to
me because I did not yet have
faith and so did not know what I
was doing.'[2] Paul was conscious
of that overwhelming sense of the
mercy of God which accepted him
as he was in his sinfulness,
redeemed him and forgave him,
appointed him an apostle of the
faith that he had once persecuted,
and commissioned him to take
that message to the Gentiles,

Paul recognised that God's
grace enabled us to be his sons
not his slaves. The grace of God
redeemed us and enabled us to
serve him. In Romans Paul
discusses the relationship between
God's grace and the elect, those
who are chosen for salvation, and
the non-elect, those who are not

so chosen. He discusses it in
relation to the choice of Jacob and
the rejection of Esau. We might
well ask at what point is an
individual ultimately responsible?[3]

Paul makes the point in
Ephesians that God has chosen the
elect not on the basis of any
worth within them, or any
achievement that they have
accomplished, but solely
according to his grace through
their faith.[4] God's mercy is such
that he chooses to save those who
believe in Christ.

The grace of God is seen at
work in the conflict within Paul
which is given exposure in
Romans 7, a conflict that we all
face:

*I do not understand what I do; for I
don't do what I would like to do,
but instead I do what I hate. Since
what I do is what I don't want to
do, this shows that I agree that the
Law is right. So I am not really the
one who does this thing; rather it is
the sin that lives in me. I know that
good does not live in me — that is,
in my human nature. For even
though the desire to do good is in
me, I am not able to do it. I don't do
the good I want to do; instead, I do
the evil that I do not want to do. If I
do what I don't want to do, this
means that I am no longer the one
who does it; instead, it is the sin that
lives in me . . . What an unhappy
man I am! Who will rescue me from
this body that is taking me to death?
Thanks be to God, who does this
through our Lord Jesus Christ!* [5]

That internal conflict within Paul
could only be answered by God's
mercy and grace. Through God's
grace he had an inner peace
through being rescued by the Lord
Jesus Christ.

'I do not claim that I have already succeeded or have already become perfect. I keep striving to win the prize for which Christ Jesus has already won me to himself. Of course, my brothers, I really do not think that I have already won it; the one thing I do, however, is to forget what is behind me and do my best to reach what is ahead.'
— PAUL in his Letter to the Philippians

(b) The preaching of the gospel
One of the main themes in Paul's ministry was his desire to fulfil God's purpose of preaching the gospel. Frequently he said similar things to the following: 'I have no right to boast just because I preach the gospel. After all, I am under orders to do so. And how terrible it would be for me if I did not preach the gospel.!'[6]

Paul believed that people by nature possess an inner moral law, an awareness of the difference between right and wrong that makes them morally responsible before God. They understand fundamental principles of behaviour and morality. They will be judged by how they have measured up to their own standards according to the light that God has given them. However, sin so influences the lives of people that there are none of us that can stand innocent before God. Even those people without the Jewish Law which clearly defines sin, know what it is to commit sin, and consequently both Jew and Gentile are accountable before God and will come under judgment. Consequently there is an inescapable missionary imperative to take the message of God to all those who would perish outside of the gospel. Paul felt the burden of the lost heavy upon his heart and he was anxious to take the good news of Jesus to every creature.

(c) The significance of weakness
Paul had great gifts of administration, outstanding organising ability and gifts of thought and speech, but these great talents and gifts could have easily led him into becoming a person who was full of self-confidence and who spent his every effort building his own private kingdom. Paul was saved from that by what he called his 'thorn in the flesh'. That physical weakness, illness or disability stopped him from being self-confident and self-reliant and instead made him depend in his weakness all the more upon God's strength. It became a unique aspect of Paul's life that out of weakness he found increased strength. As he said, '. . . to keep me from being puffed up with pride because of the many wonderful things I saw, I was given a painful physical ailment, which acts as Satan's messenger to beat and keep me from being proud.'[7] That particular 'painful physical ailment', the nature of which we do not know, was a persistent problem which prayer failed to remove. However, that weakness became a strength:

Three times I prayed to the Lord about this and asked him to take it away. But his answer was: 'My grace is all you need, for my power is greatest when you are weak.' I am most happy, then, to be proud of my weaknesses, in order to feel the protection of Christ's power over me. I am content with weaknesses, insults, hardships, persecutions, and difficulties for Christ's sake. For when I am weak, then I am strong.[8]

It is impossible to understand the nature of Paul's tremendous achievement without acknowledging the significance of weakness within his life.

Paul saw this paradox as one of the great insights in God's relationship with men. The cross itself was paradoxical, for what was the sign of rejection with men was the sign of acceptance with God. The cross was evidence of futility, but because of God's grace it became the great symbol of man's future. What was the sign of guilt became the emblem of innocence. What was man's greatest folly was in reality part of the wisdom of God. What was an emblem of sin became the means of forgiveness. Jesus was the stone rejected by the builders, whom God in his grace made the cornerstone of a new temple.

Out of Paul's own experience, and the example of what happened on the cross of Calvary, Paul came to an understanding of how God works through human weakness to achieve his purposes.

(d) The love of people
Paul could become angry with those who were hurting the cause of Christ, yet overriding this was his compassion and love for people. Paul had compassion for those who had been redeemed. He had compassion for those who were yet outside the faith. He even had compassion for those who were opposing the faith.

Paul found it possible to so love others that love became the basic motive in all that he did. For them he was willing to abase himself rather than offend a brother, and went without wife and family in order to be free to serve others. As already mentioned, that love for people could be seen in the very generous way Paul spoke about those who served with him. It extended to all races and social and economic conditions, and no one was outside his circle of care: 'so we preach Christ to everyone. With

all possible wisdom we warn everyone and teach them in order to bring each one into God's presence as a mature individual in union with Christ.'[9]

(e) The future hope
One of the dominant themes in all that Paul wrote and spoke about was his hope in the future. He was confident because he was 'in Christ' and was caught up with the cosmic victory of Christ. Each individual Christian was not on his own in the struggle of life, but was incorporated into the cosmic Christ to whom God had given the victory. There was nothing now in all creation that 'will ever be able to separate us from the love of God which is ours through Christ Jesus our Lord.'[11] Paul knew the victory was already assured and that because Christians were incorporated 'in Christ' they were already sharing that victory.

(f) The living Christ
The meeting with the resurrected Christ on the Damascus road was the most momentous event in the life of Paul. To actually meet him whom he knew to be crucified and to hear his voice coming from the blinding light saying 'I am Jesus'[11] made such a profound impact that his life was completely turned around. To him Christ was the living head of the church, and believers had a part to play as they functioned as his body taking his message into the world. He referred to the church as the body of Christ, the community of saints, brethren together and the true Israel. The believers are the divine gathering of the future already established here on earth. Christ is so intimately involved in the church

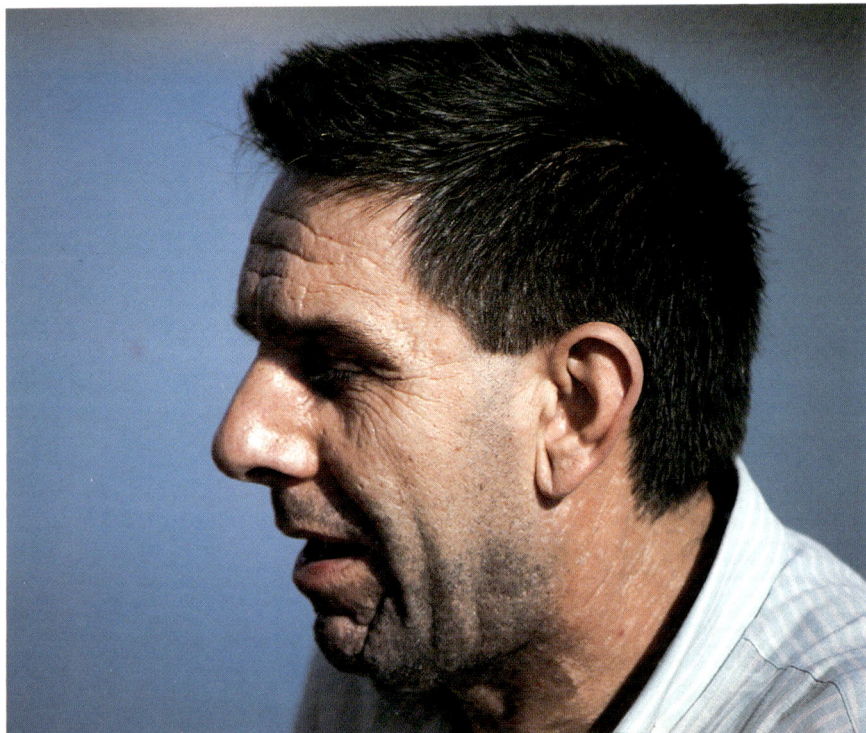

that its suffering becomes his own and in a mysterious sense completes his own suffering.

(g) The transformed life
Paul's idea of the transformed life is that we live no longer according to the flesh, but according to the Spirit. Paul knew what it was to experience the ecstasy of the presence and the gifts and graces of the Holy Spirit. He claimed to have a number of gifts of the Holy Spirit including apostleship, prophecy, the ability to speak in tongues, healing and teaching. Paul mentions approximately twenty gifts from the Holy Spirit to enable the believer to witness and praise more effectively. These spiritual gifts were special abilities given by God to Christians. There were some similarities between spiritual gifts and natural talents as both come from God and may be used for godly purposes. But the Christian may also possess a distinctive gift from the Holy Spirit. The Holy Spirit also gave graces, or 'the fruit of the Spirit'. Paul lists these qualities of character that Christians should develop when we live by the Spirit.

The Christian is to exercise the gifts of the Holy Spirit and to evidence the fruit of the Holy Spirit. Already each Christian has been given both gifts and graces but yet we must strive to develop them within us. The Christian already is a new-born person, but he must strive to become what he already is.

Paul's significance today

How can we adequately assess the contemporary significance of Paul? His theology is basic to all that is Christian. His life has inspired generations. His example of a life turned round and thoroughly committed to Jesus Christ has inspired men and women to give themselves into the service of the Master. His journeys and epistles have been the means whereby we have understood how the church has grown, and what it is that we believe. Paul looked into the depths of man's condition and explained how God in his grace and mercy reached into our depths of sin and restored and renewed us.

In other centuries men have been inclined to scoff at the writings of Paul as a narrow-minded fanatical Jew who took the beautiful, simple, clear, homespun philosophies of Jesus and turned them into a religion about Jesus. However, people today do not make that distinction, for scholars will not allow that slur to be made.

In twentieth-century secularism, there is a need for self-confident and self-satisfied people to really understand their true nature and to discover the resources and salvation from God. The terms Paul uses do not belong to the ancient world, but reach across the centuries and touch the deepest needs of people. We might become smug as our communication satellites circle the universe and our computers make calculations faster than the mind can think, but we still do not know how to handle our own guilt or to relate to those we love. To our deepest and most permanent need, the word of God through the apostle Paul speaks clearly.

The early church gave their verdict on the life of the apostle Paul when his epistles — ordinary letters written to ordinary Christians in ordinary cities about ordinary problems — were collected and circulated by them and immediately regarded as being inspired by God. In all of history, Paul is second in the story of the church only to his Master. He is the outstanding ambassador for Christ. He still stands high above the others, pointing always to Jesus Christ.

For personal reading

Theme: Faithfulness to Christ

MONDAY | Spiritual struggle
Romans 7:13-25

TUESDAY | Christian ethics
Romans 12:3-13

WEDNESDAY | Warning against worldly contention
2 Corinthians 10:1-6

THURSDAY | The weak made strong
2 Corinthians 12:7-10

FRIDAY | Travelling with the gospel
2 Corinthians 8:16-24

SATURDAY | To live in Christ
Philippians 1:15-16

SUNDAY | Suffering for Christ
Romans 5:1-11

For group study

Topic: Being complete in Christ

1 What is most important to you in life?

2 Do you have a personal and meaningful relationship with Jesus Christ? What did Paul mean when he emphasised a personal life 'in Christ'?

3 People felt Paul's tremendous influence by his visits, speeches and writings. In what ways are you an influence for good on others?

4 'While we were yet sinners Christ died for us.' What can God's grace and mercy mean to us?

5 In what ways do you cope with weakness and suffering? Can God make any difference?

6 How can we discover our own God-given gifts and graces?

7 What have you discovered about Paul, his life, and his ministry?

End notes

Chapter 1:
Paul the Pharisee

1 Philemon 1-2
2 See Romans 1:8-15;
   15:14-33
3 Romans 16:22
4 1 Corinthians 16:21; 2
   Thessalonians 3:17
5 1 Corinthians 13
6 Philippians 2:5-11
7 2 Timothy 1:11-13
8 Romans 12:9-13;
   Philippians 4:8-9
9 See, for example, Acts
   16:16-17; 20:5-15;
   21:1-18; 27:1-28
10 Acts 1:1-4; Luke 1:1-4
11 See Acts 6:7; 12:24;
   16:5; 19:20
12 Acts 20:34
13 Galatians 1:15, using
   Jeremiah 1:5
14 Philippians 3:6
15 Acts 22:28
16 Acts 21:39
17 Acts 5:38
18 Malachi 3:16-17
19 Acts 9:29
20 Acts 26:9-11

Chapter 2:
Paul the Persecutor

1 1 Corinthians 15:3-8
2 C.H. Dodd, *The
   Apostolic Preaching
   and Its Development*,
   Hodder and Stoughton,
   1936, pp.21-24
3 Acts 1:8
4 J.B. Phillips,
   Introduction to *Letters
   to Young Churches*,
   Geoffrey Bles, 1955,
   p.xiv
5 Acts 6:14
6 Acts 17:6
7 Acts 4:1-3

8 E.M. Blaiklock, *The
   Archaeology of the
   New Testament*,
   Thomas Nelson, 1984,
   p.140
9 Acts 4:19-20
10 Acts 5:40-42
11 Acts 6:14
12 Mark 14:57-58
13 Leviticus 24:14
14 Acts 7:58b and 8:1
15 Acts 8:1-3
16 Acts 26:9-11
17 Philippians 3:6
18 Acts 9:3-6
19 2 Corinthians 4:5-6
20 Galatians 1:15
21 Acts 9:15-16
22 Acts 9:17
23 2 Corinthians 5:17-19
24 1 Corinthians 9:1
25 1 Corinthians 15:8
26 Galatians 1:18-19
27 A.M. Hunter, *The
   Gospel According to St
   Paul*, SCM, 1966,
   pp.59-60
28 Charles W. Colson,
   Life Sentence, Hodder
   and Stoughton, 1979,
   pp.148-149
29 John Perkins, *With
   Justice for All*, Regal
   Books, 1982, pp.18-19
30 Sir John Betjeman,
   'The Conversion of St
   Paul' in *Collected
   Poems*, Murray, 1971,
   p.87
31 Acts 9:24-25
32 Galatians 1:18
33 Acts 9:29-31
34 Acts 9:31

Chapter 3:
Paul the Preacher

1 Acts 20:7-12
2 Acts 9:20

3 Acts 13:13-43
4 Acts 19:8-10
5 Acts 17:16-38
6 1 Corinthians 1:20-24
7 Romans 1:16-17
8 Ephesians 2:7-9
9 Romans 5:20-21
10 Romans 3:22-26
11 Charles Colson, 'Ten
   Years after Watergate',
   in *Christianity Today*,
   1985
12 Romans 5:12-21
13 Romans 1:18-32
14 Romans 3:21-22
15 Romans 5:16-18
16 J. Calvin, *Commentary
   on the Epistle of Paul
   the Apostle to the
   Romans*, Collected
   Works,
17 Ephesians 4:13
18 1 Corinthians 1:25-30
19 Romans 8:7
20 Romans 6:1-2
21 Romans 6:16-18
22 Philippians 2:12-13
23 Romans 8:24
24 2 Corinthians 15:2
25 Romans 5:9
26 Romans 5:1-2
27 Ephesians 2:12-16
28 Romans 1:17
29 Joel 2:28
30 Ephesians 1:13-14

Chapter 4:
Paul the Pastor

1 Ephesians 4:11
2 1 Kings 19:4
3 Acts 9:23-24
4 Acts 9:29
5 1 Corinthians 15:32
6 2 Corinthians 11:23-28
7 Acts 13:13-14
8 Philippians 1:3-7
9 Galatians 4:11,19
10 Acts 14:21

11 Romans 15:19-24
12 2 Corinthians 10:10
13 E.A. Judge, *Cultural Conformity and Innovation in Paul: some clues from contemporary documents*, The Tyndale Bulletin 35, 1984
14 Acts 15:36-40
15 Acts 17:16
16 Acts 3:1-26
17 Acts 14:8-11,19
18 Philippians 2:27
19 Acts 9:26
20 1 Corinthians 9:5-6
21 Romans 11:13
22 Acts 20:24
23 Romans 15:15-17
24 2 Corinthians 12:9-10
25 Philippians 2:17
26 2 Corinthians 4:8-9,16
27 1 Thessalonians 2:9; 2 Thessalonians 3:7-8
28 1 Corinthians 2:1-5
29 2 Corinthians 10:13-15
30 1 Corinthians 9:24-27
31 Acts 20:36-38
32 2 Corinthians 5:6,8
33 1 Corinthians 10:13
34 Acts 18:5-6

Chapter 5:
Paul the Pioneer

1 These statistics are from David B. Barrett (ed.), *World Christian Encyclopedia*, OUP, 1982
2 Acts 26:20
3 Romans 16:26
4 Acts 5:30-32
5 Acts 10:34-35
6 Acts 9:15
7 1 Corinthians 9:19-22
8 Acts 13:2
9 Romans 15:18
10 Galatians 2:6-10
11 Acts 16:10
12 Acts 16:11-15
13 Philippians 4:3
14 Hebrews 12:2

Chapter 6:
Paul the Protagonist

1 Acts 22:1
2 James 1:27
3 Philippians 1:15-17

4 Galatians 3:5
5 Romans 6:14
6 Luke 22:20
7 Acts 15:7-11
8 Acts 15:20
9 1 Corinthians 8:6
10 Romans 5:8-9
11 Colossians 1:15-17
12 Philippians 2:6-11
13 1 Corinthians 2:2
14 2 Corinthians 5:18-19
15 Romans 6:4
16 Ephesians 1:19-20
17 J.I. Packer, in J. Buchanan, *The Doctrine of Justification*, Banner of Truth Trust, 1984 reprint, Introduction p.vii
18 Romans 1:16-17
19 Ephesians 1:5
20 Romans 8:14-21
21 1 Timothy 2:5-6
22 Romans 3:25
23 Romans 8:22-23
24 Romans 5:1
25 1 Corinthians 6:11
26 1 Thessalonians 4:8
27 2 Corinthians 1:21-22
28 2 Corinthians 1:22
29 Romans 8:26
30 Romans 8:10
31 1 Corinthians 1:2
32 1 Corinthians 12:27
33 Ephesians 5:22-27
34 Ephesians 2:19-21
35 John 9:25

Chapter 7:
Paul the Philosopher

1 Galatians 2:11-14
2 Acts 13:10-11
3 Acts 13:45
4 Acts 24:5-9
5 Acts 15:1-2
6 Philippians 3:18-19
7 Acts 17:18
8 Acts 6:1-2
9 1 Corinthians 15:32
10 John 1:1-3;14
11 Acts 17:16-34
12 Acts 17:22-23
13 Acts 17:26-28
14 Acts 17:30-31
15 Acts 17:32-34

Chapter 8:
Paul the Patriot

1 Yigael Yadin, *Masada — Herod's Fortress and the Zealots' Last Stand*, Steimatsky, Jerusalem, 1984, pp.224-230
2 Matthew 27:25
3 Stan Telchin, *Betrayed!*, Marshall, Morgan & Scott, London, 1981, p.25
4 Philippians 3:5-7
5 Romans 9:2-5
6 Romans 11:16-17
7 Romans 11:17-18, 24
8 Romans 1:16
9 Acts 13:45-47
10 Romans 1:16
11 Romans 2:7-9
12 Romans 2:10
13 Matthew 21:33-43
14 Acts 4:13
15 Deuteronomy 21:22-23
16 Romans 19:1-4
17 Romans 11:1-12
18 Stan Telchin, *Betrayed!*, Marshall, Morgan & Scott, London, 1981, pp.117-118

Chapter 9:
Paul the Proclaimer

1 2 Samuel 22:47
2 Luke 9:60
3 Acts 4:31
4 1 Corinthians 1:23-24
5 1 Corinthians 10:10
6 1 Corinthians 1:17; 2:1,4
7 Michael Green, *Evangelism in the Early Church*, Eerdmans, Grand Rapids, 1970, p.54
8 Philippians 3:18
9 Acts 20:23-24
10 1 Corinthians 7:1;8:1
11 Ephesians 1:1
12 Philippians 2:25-30
13 Philemon 2; Romans 16:13
14 Romans 10:5;16:8-9;16:12
15 Romans 3:22-23
16 Ephesians 2:11-16
17 Galatians 3:28
18 1 Corinthians 11:5
19 1 Corinthians 11:13-16

20 Philippians 4:2-3
21 1 Corinthians 3:5; 2
 Corinthians 3:6; 1
 Corinthians 16:15
22 Romans 16:1-2
23 Romans 16:7
24 Philemon 15-17

10 1 Corinthians 16:22
11 1 Corinthians 15:51-54
12 Philippians 2:10-11
13 1 Corinthians 4:5
14 Colossians 1:20
15 2 Corinthians 5:1-4
16 1 Corinthians 11:26

10 Acts 26:31
11 Acts 28:14
12 Philippians 4:22
13 Philippians 1:12-13
14 Tacitus, *Annals*, Book
 XV, 44
15 2 Timothy 4:6-8

Chapter 10:
Paul the Prophet

1 Matthew 25:1-13;
 Revelation 21
2 Acts 9:1-16
3 Acts 17:30
4 Romans 1-2
5 1 Thessalonians 5:23
6 1 Corinthians 3:21-23
7 1 Thessalonians 4:15-17
8 Romans 8:23
9 John 14:3; Matthew
 25:31

Chapter 11:
Paul the Prisoner

1 Acts 16:37-39
2 2 Corinthians 11:24-25
3 2 Timothy 4:9-13
4 1 Corinthians 15:32
5 1 Corinthians 16:9
6 2 Corinthians 1:8-10
7 Acts 21:27
8 Tacitus: *History*, 5:9,
 Sir Ronald Syme
 (trans.), OUP, 1958
9 Acts 24:27

Chapter 12:
Paul the Person

1 Acts 14:20-21
2 1 Timothy 1:13
3 Romans 9:10-18
4 Ephesians 2:8-9
5 Romans 7:15-25
6 1 Corinthians 9:16
7 2 Corinthians 12:7
8 2 Corinthians 12:8-10
9 Colossians 1:28
10 Romans 8:39
11 Acts 22:8

Bibliography

Author	Title	Publisher	Place	Date
Aksit Ilhan	*Ancient Civilisations of Anatolia and Historic Treasures of Turkey*	Aksit Kuttur	Ankara	1983
Aksit Ilhan	*The Civilisation of Western Anatolia*	Aksit Kuttur	Ankara	1984
Aksit Ilhan	*Haghis Sophia Kariye Museum*	Aksit Kuttur	Istanbul	1984
Aksit Ilhan	*Topkapi*	Aksit Kuttur	Ankara	1984
Akurgal Ekrem	*Ancient Civilisations and Ruins of Turkey*	Kitabeyi	Istanbul	1983
Banks Robert	*Paul's Idea of Community*	Anzea	Sydney	1979
Baran Dr Musa	*Cappadocia*	Nature	Izmir	1984
Baran Dr Musa	*Meander Valley From Priene to Hierapolis*	Molay	Izmir	1984
Baran Dr Musa	*Pergamum*	Ticaret	Izmir	1984
Barclay William	*The Mind of St Paul*	Fontana	London	1965
Barratt C.K. (ed)	*The New Testament Background: Selected Documents*	Harper	New York	1974
Blouet Brian	*The Story of Malta*			
Blaiklock E.M. and Harrison R.K.	*Dictionary of Biblical Archaeology*	Zondervan	Grand Rapids	1983
Blaiklock E.M.	*The Archaeology of the New Testament*	Thomas Nelson	New York	1984
Blaiklock E.M.	*The World of the New Testament*	Harper	London	1979
Blaiklock E.M.	*The New International Dictionary of Biblical Archaeology*	Zondervan	Grand Rapids	1983
Blake Everett C. & Edmonds Anna G.	*Biblical Sites in Turkey*	Redhouse Press	Istanbul	1982
Bornkamn G.	*Paul*	Harper & Row	London	1971
Bruce F.F.	*Apostle of the Free Spirit*	Paternoster	Exeter	1977
Bruce F.F.	*The Book of the Acts (New International Commentary on the New Testament)*	Eerdmans	Grand Rapids	various dates
Bruce F.F.	*Men and Movements in The Primitive Church*	Paternoster	Exeter	1979
Bruce F.F.	*New Testament History*	Doubleday	New York	1972
Bruce F.F.	*Places They Knew: Jesus and Paul*	Ark	London	1981
Bruce F.F.	*Jesus and Christian Origins Outside the New Testament*	Hodder	London	1981

Author	Title	Publisher	Place	Date
Bruce F.F.	*The Pauline Circle*	Paternoster	Exeter	1985
Buttrick George Arthur (ed)	*The Interpreter's Dictionary of the Bible (5 volumes)*	Abingdon	Nashville	1976
Cimok Faith	*Antioch on the Orontes*	Tanitma Merkezi	Ankara	1980
Coggan Donald	*Paul, Portrait of a Revolutionary*	Hodder and Stoughton	Kent	1984
Delicostopoulos Dr Alan	*St Paul's Journey to Greece and Cyprus*	Efstathiadis	Athens	1979
Dodd C.H.	*The Meaning of Paul for Today*	Hodder and Stoughton	London	1920
Dodd C.H.	*The Apostolic Preaching and its development*	Hodder and Stoughton	London	1936
Douglas J.D. et al. (eds)	*The Illustrated Bible Dictionary*	IVP	Leicester	1980
Douglas J.D. et al.	*New Testament History*	Nelson	New York	1972
Douskou Iris	*Athens — The City and its Museums*	Ekdotike Athenon	Athens	1985
Drane John	*The Life of the Early Church*	Lion	Tring	1982
Drane John	*Paul*	Lion	Tring	1976
Eliades G.S.	*The House of Dionysus The Villa of the Mosaics in New Paphos*			
Foakes-Jackson F.J.	*The Life of St Paul*	Hodder	London	1926
Goldsworthy Graeme	*The Gospel in Revelation*	Lancer Books	Australia	1984
Goreme G.	*Cappadocia*	Guzelgoz	Neveshir	1979
Goreme G.	*The Spectacular Miracles of the Past in Asia Minor*			
Green Michael	*Evangelism in the Early Church*	Eerdmans	Grand Rapids	1970
Guidebook	*Masada: Pictorial Guide and Souvenir*			
Guidebook	*The Catacombs of Rome and the Origins of Christianity*	U. Fasola	Scala	1980
Guidebook	*The Vatican Museums Scala*	de Savena	Rome	1983
Guidebook	*The Athenian Agora*	Ekdotike	Athens	1976
Guidebook	*Hagia Sophia (Istanbul Mosque)*	NET	Istanbul	1984
Guthrie Donald	*New Testament Introduction*	IVP	London	1970
Hunter A.M.	*The Gospel According to St Paul*	SCM	London	1966
Jones M.	*St Paul the Orator*	Hodder and Stoughton	London	1910
Josephus	*Antiquities of the Jews and Jewish Wars*	Harvard Uni.	Harvard	1926
Kerr H. and Mulder J.	*Conversions*	Hodder and Stoughton	London	1984
Klausner J.	*The Messianic Idea in Israel*	Macmillan	Basingstoke	1965
Knox J.	*Chapters in a Life of Paul*	Abingdon	Nashville	1950
McDowell J.	*Evidence that Demands a Verdict*	Campus Crusade	Arrowhead Springs	1972

Author	Title	Publisher	Place	Date
Meinardus Otto	St John of Patmos and the Seven Churches of the Apocalypse	Lycabettus Press	Athens	1974
Meinardus Otto	St Paul in Ephesus and the Cities of Galatia and Cyprus	Lycabettus Press	Athens	1973
Meinardus Otto	St Paul in Greece	Lycabettus Press	Athens	1973
Meyer F.B.	Paul: Servant of Jesus	Lakeland (reprint)	London	1968
Morris G.	The Mystery and Meaning of Christian Conversion	World Methodist Council	Nashville	1981
Morton H.V.	In the Steps of St Paul	Methuen	London	1936
Muggeridge M. and Vidler A.	Paul: Envoy Extraordinary	Collins	London	1972
Onen Dr U.	Ephesus, Ruins and Museum The City's History through Art	Akademia	Izmir	1983
Packer, Tenney and White (eds)	The World of the New Testament	Nelson	Nashville	1982
Packer, Tenney and White (eds)	The Bible Almanac	Nelson	Nashville	1980
Papathanasso- poulis G.	The Acropolis Monuments and Museums	Krene	Athens	1977
Papahatzis N.	Ancient Corinth	Ekdotike Athenon	Athens	1984
Petsas P.	Delphi	Krene	Athens	1981
Phillips J.B.	Letters to the Young Churches	Geoffrey Bles	London	1947
Plurigraf	Rome and Vatican New Coloured Guide Book	Bonechi	Rome	1984
Plurigraf	The Roman Forum New Coloured Guide Book	Bonechi	Rome	1984
Provatakis Theo	Meteora	Toubi's		
Ramsay W.M.	St Paul: The Traveller and Roman Citizen	Hodder and Stoughton	London	1896
Ramsay W.M.	The Letters to the Seven Churches	Hodder and Stoughton	London	1904
Sanders J.O.	Paul the Leader	Kingsway	Eastbourne	1983
Stevenson J. (ed)	A New Eusebius	SPCK	London	1968
Stewart J.S.	A Man in Christ: Vital Elements of St Paul's Religion	Hodder and Stoughton	London	1935
Tasker R.V.G.	James (Tyndale New Testament Commentaries)	Tyndale	London	1957
Telchin S.	Betrayed!	Marshall Morgan & Scott	London	1981
Tenney Merrill C.	New Testament Times	Nelson	London	1965
Themelis Petros G.	Ancient Corinth The Site and the Museum	Hanibal	Athens	1984
Thompson Homer A.	The Athenian Agora A Guide to the Excavation and Museum	American School of Classics	Athens	1976

Author		Publisher	Place	Date
Unger Merrill F.	*Archaeology and the New Testament*	Eerdmans	Grand Rapids	1962
Wallis J.	*The Call to Conversion*	Lion	Tring	1981
Yadin Y.	*Masada*	Steinmatzky	Tel Aviv	1984
Yamauchi E.	*The World of the First Christians*	Lion	Tring	1981
Yamauchi E	*The First Photographs of Jerusalem The Old City*	Ariel Publishing	Jerusalem	1976
Yamauchi E.	*Michelangelo & Raphael in The Vatican*	Pietrangeli	Rome	1980

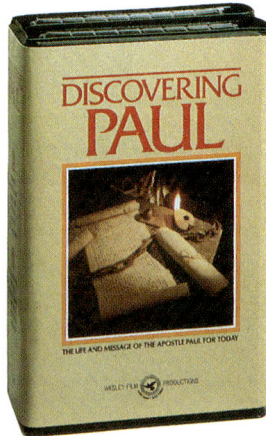

Video cassettes

This book is based on the twelve-part film series, *Discovering Paul*, originally screened on major television networks in Australia and available on video. For further details of the video series, please write to:

TRA Productions
Wesley Central Mission
210 Pitt Street
Sydney, NSW 2000
Australia

Phone (02) 267 8741

All Bible passages are from the *Good News Bible* (American Bible Society edition).